THE HISTORY OF PRESCOT GRAMMAR SCHOOL AND PRESCOT SCHOOL

1544 - 1994

THE HISTORY OF
PRESCOT GRAMMAR SCHOOL
AND PRESCOT SCHOOL

1544 - 1994

FRANCIS A BAILEY M.A.
et al.

450th Anniversary Edition

Edited by
J SIDNEY BAILIE

FVTVRAM   CIVITATEM   INQVIRIMVS

THE   OLD   PRESCOTIAN

First edition	1944
Second edition	1971
Third (revised) edition	1993

ISBN 0 952 1407 05

Published by
The Old Prescotian
Prescot School, Prescot, Merseyside.
Copyright Prescot School 1993
Printed in Great Britain by
Flexipress, Ormskirk.

British Library Cataloguing-in-Publication Data.
A catalogue record for this book is available from the British Library.

THE COAT OF ARMS OF
PRESCOT GRAMMAR SCHOOL

For many years Prescot Grammar School had adopted, together with the town itself, the Arms of King's College, Cambridge, Lords of the Manor of Prescot. In 1933 the College of Arms issued Letters Patent granting its own armorial bearings to the School. Based on those borne by the family of the Founder, the ancient Lancashire House of Lathom, the school arms were differenced by the additional charge of an open Book symbolising Education. In the crest the Eagle is preserved but with a Torch symbolising Progress held in its dexter claw.   The motto, *FVTVRAM CIVITATEM INQVIRIMVS* (We seek the State that is to be or We seek a New Community) is derived from the preamble to the founder's will, "I, Gilbert Lathum, preist, calling to remembraunce the sentance of Saynte Paule (ad Hebraos) non habemus his civitatem menentem sed futuram inquirimus".

F.A. Bailey

The Authors

FRANCIS ARTHUR BAILEY was born in 1904 at Lutterworth, Leicestershire, and received his early education at Aldershot High School. He later attended King Alfred College, Winchester, and took his B.A. degree in the University of London in 1925. Six years later he obtained his M.A., Class One with Distinction, in London. He joined the staff of Prescot Grammar School as history master in 1926.
F.A. Bailey was a founder of Prescot Historical Society and made Prescot the scene of his life's activities. He unearthed many historic aspects of the town which otherwise would have been lost. A prolific writer, he was the author of numerous books and pamphlets and he contributed to many learned journals. Only two weeks before his death he completed his definitive *History of Southport,* a work researched in great depth and which was reprinted in 1992 by Sefton Libraries. 'Frank' Bailey was a member of the Historical Society of Lancashire and Cheshire, the Lancashire Parish Records Society as well as many local organisations and committees. For a period he was a lecturer in the Extra-Mural Department of the University of Liverpool.
A quiet man of dry wit, 'Fab' died suddenly in 1955 at the age of fifty-one.

Geoffrey DIXON, B.A., London, joined the English department of Prescot Grammar School in 1927. He became Senior English Master, Deputy Head and eventually Acting Head before retiring in 1969. He retained his interest in the School and served as a Foundation Governor for several years.

John C.S. WEEKS, C.B.E., M.A., Cantab. was Head of Prescot Grammar School from 1968 until 1977.

Peter A. BARLOW, B.A., B.Mus., Leeds, was appointed to the Headship of Prescot School in 1977.

E. Barbara SMITH, B.A., Liverpool, was the second Head of Prescot Girls' Grammar School, 1968 - 1977.

A. John WILLMOTT, PhD., Manchester, a former pupil of the School (43-53), is a senior lecturer in Computer Science in the University of York.

W.J. 'Bill' SHEILS, PhD., is Provost of Goodricke College in the University of York and former Director of the Borthwick Institute for Historical Research, York.

The Bringing-up of Youth

"No learning ought to be learned with bondage, for bodily labours wrought by compulsion hurt not the body, but any learning learnt by compulsion tarrieth not long in the mind. And why?

For whatsoever the mind doth learn unwillingly with fear, the same it doth quickly forget without care... ... ... Fond schoolmasters neither can understand nor will follow this good counsel of Socrates, but wise riders, in their office, can and will do both; which is the only cause that commonly the young gentlemen of England go so unwillingly to school and run so fast to the stable.

For in very deed fond schoolmasters, by fear, do beat unto them the hatred of learning, and wise riders, by gentle allurement, do breed up in them the love of riding. They find fear and bondage in schools; they feel liberty and freedom in stables; which causeth them utterly to abhor the one and most gladly to haunt the other."

"The Scholemaster" 1570 by Roger Ascham

From The Rt. Hon. The Earl of Derby, M.C.

Knowsley
Prescot
Merseyside
L34 4AF

I am delighted to think that many of my forebears have been associated with the School since its foundation.

It is inevitable that having been in existence for 450 years, the School has suffered many vicissitudes during its long life, but by wise management and determination, and with the assistance of many benefactors, the successive governing bodies and headmasters have succeeded in maintaining its proud traditions.

The country has seen great changes even in this century. Prescot is a totally different town and the School has become a Comprehensive establishment.

From the Chairman of Governors,
Gary Cheesman

MY time as Chairman of Governors of Prescot School has been one of great uncertainty within the Education System; the National Curriculum and Local Management of Schools have brought inevitable difficulties. The School is celebrating 450 years of overcoming difficulties; a wonderful testament to those responsible for its past stewardship and something of a comfort when struggling with the problems of today.

Over those 450 years, the School has built a formidable reputation founded not on its financial strength or its buildings (although these are the focus of much needed attention at present) but on people dedicated to the provision of sound education and solid values which are just as important now, at the end of the twentieth century, as they were in the middle of the sixteenth.

It is that group of committed individuals; in a multitude of roles, paid and unpaid; who ensure that young people from the area leave the School, just as they have for four and a half centuries, well educated and equipped to make their personal mark in the World, each according to their own ability.

I am honoured to be associated with that team and delighted to have this opportunity to thank them formally and encourage them to even greater efforts in the work of building the future.

> *"Time present and time past*
> *'Are both perhaps present in time future,*
> *'And time future contained in time past."*
>
> Thomas Stearns Eliot 1888 - 1965

Sincere thanks are due particularly to J.S. *'Pat'* Bailie for his sterling work in the preparation of this volume which will now become part of the rich history that is Prescot School.

From the Chairman of Foundation Governors,
The Rev. Thomas M. Steel

AS Vicar of Prescot and Chairman of Foundation Governors of Prescot School it gives me the greatest pleasure to introduce this new edition of the School's history, now published by Old Boys of the School.

I am keenly aware of the close involvement of my predecessors in office with the School and its affairs from the very beginning and it has been a privilege to join in that tradition. Indeed, I have perhaps all the more reason to do so for I hope to prove before too long that my ancestor, Andrew Lathum of Whiston who died in 1570, was closely related to our honoured Founder.

The School has changed in countless ways since 1544 as it has reflected shifting philosophies of education and the rich history and varying fortunes of our town. I like to think that the provision of free education (which was the keystone of Gilbert Lathum's plan) and that commitment to excellence, for which the School has been so justly famed in the years which have followed, can together make the School's next hundred years an equally impressive chapter.

I am sure that the goodwill of many distinguished and loyal former pupils who are drawn together by the anniversary celebrations will be a vital element in ensuring this continuity.

Those of us who are most closely associated with Prescot and its School want to be sure that the proud traditions so rightly celebrated this year are used as a strength on which today's School and tomorrow's town may draw.

I send my thanks and warmest good wishes to all who have worked so hard to ensure the success of the great events of 1994.

SPONSORSHIP

THE publication of this work would not have been possible but for the financial support of our Sponsors. Their generosity has enabled all the income from the sale of the book to be credited directly to the school fund. We owe a deep debt of gratitude to them all, especially to

The Rt. Hon the Earl of Derby, MC.,
BICC Components, Prescot,
Pilkington plc, St Helens,
Tyrers Ltd., Department Store, St Helens,
Prescot School Foundation Governors.

The Rt. Hon. the Earl of Derby, M.C.
The Chairman of Governors, Mr Gary Cheesman
The Chairman of Foundation Governors, The Rev. Thomas M. Steel

The Sponsors

CONTENTS

"Futuram Civitatem Inquirimus"
C.W.H. Richardson, M.A.,

PREFACE

Part 1 : 1544 - 1944
F.A. Bailey

Part 2 : 1944 - 1994
G. Dixon   J.C.S.Weeks   P.A. Barlow

Appendix

FVTVRAM CIVITATEM INQVIRIMVS
(We Seek After A State To Come)

From an Introduction to the First Edition by Mr C.W.H. Richardson, M.A.,
Headmaster, 1908 - 1937

The governors and members of the staff must have chosen for Prescot Grammar School the above motto, taken out of a quotation from Hebrews XIII, 14, in the will of its Founder, Gilbert Lathum, with confidence in their choice that the school would play its part in years to come in endeavouring to maintain and also to enhance the greatness of the reputation of the town of Prescot. Using the meaning of the word *"Civitatem"* in its widest significance, let us consider how the town of Prescot has "sought after a state to come" and incidentally how its Grammar School has endeavoured to play its part in helping to bring about the result.

How has the school endeavoured to carry out its motto? There was a time not long ago when the school of fifty boys was run by one man, the late Mr. J. Scholfield. All honour to him for his work in keeping, single-handed, the "school" in being under most difficult conditions. Although many of his pupils did not remain with him long after their fourteenth birthday, nevertheless in after life they obtained positions of distinction in many callings. Today the school has 400 pupils with a fully qualified and comptetent staff and an Old Boys' Association, which never fails to foster the interests of its old school in every way.

It was during the Great War, 1914-1918, that the school was housed in five separate buildings in the town, and at the end of the war, plans drawn up by the County Architect were laid before the governors for the building of a new school at a cost of over £50,000 - then the "Axe" came and the present buildings of a semi-permanent character - at about half the cost - had to be substituted in the grounds on St. Helens Road, so generously sold to the Lancashire County Council, at a nominal figure, by the Right Honourable the Earl of Derby.

At that time and for many years afterwards the boys who stayed for dinner were few and their dining room also served the purpose of cloak room and physics laboratory - their sole equipment for the meal was a kettle, kindly supplied by the parents of four brothers. To-day more than 160 boys sit down for a well served mid-day meal in a comfortable dining room. In the 'old school' two wash-basins had to serve 260 boys and the method of heating was by coke stoves - to say nothing of the need of a pair of pliers to turn the gas taps.

The school has produced many excellent athletes, although many Old Boys will remember it had no playing fields of its own; but in this year of the Quatercentenary of its Foundation it has won handsomely the Liverpool Schools' Shield - no mean honour - against powerful opponents from Liverpool schools.

There have been times in the history of the school when its very existence has been threatened. Once, the governors had to put their hands in their own pockets to save the situation, and Mr. W.A. Cross, the Secretary to the Governors, will well remember a time when the Balance Sheet at the end of a financial year showed a balance of under six pounds. Once, a sub-committee of the Lancashire Education Committee came to Prescot in force to persuade the Governors that the school had outlived its usefulness and that it should be closed and its endowments used to enable boys to attend schools either in Liverpool or St. Helens, but to this proposal the Governors under the Chairmanship of Canon H. Mitchell would not agree. Under the present regime there is no doubt but that the ancient Foundation of Prescot Grammar School can look forward to a prosperous future and that its pupils will continue to "seek after a state to come."

In conclusion, I wish to say that it has been a unique opportunity for me to have the honour and the privilege to make the above contribution to this book, written to commemorate the Quatercentenary of the Foundation of Prescot Grammar School.

PREFACE TO THE THIRD EDITION

AT the suggestion of their former English master, Mr Geoffrey Dixon, three Old Boys embarked with him upon the preparation of this revised edition of the school history which had been written by F.A. Bailey in 1944 to mark the 400th Anniversary of the school's foundation. Professor J.A. Taylor, Mr A.R. Whitaker and the editor joined in what proved to be a most pleasurable task since all had enjoyed close connections with the author. Francis Bailey and Geoffrey Dixon had been colleagues for many years and the rest were their pupils more than fifty years ago. Appropriately, this third edition will be published during the year of the 450th Annivesary.

The whole of Bailey's original work which chronicles the first four hundred years of the school's history remains unedited in Part 1 of this edition. In Part 2 the fifty years following the Quatercentenary have been described by G. Dixon, J.C.S. Weeks and P.A. Barlow. E. Barbara Smith has contributed a section on the short but nonetheless important history of Prescot Girls' Grammar School. Tribute must be paid to these associate authors for their co-operation in combining differing styles into a unified whole. Certain sections of the earlier editions, not from the pen of Bailey, have been omitted as of little topical interest. To avoid interruption of the principal narrative, subsidiary material has been collected in an appendix The format of the first edition is retained throughout.

Part of the work of an editor is to secure and dispose the co-operation of experts in various disciplines. Mrs Olga Hignett, secretary at Prescot School and her staff have been unfailing in their courtesy and co-operation while Miss Helen Ford, archivist and manager of the Local Studies Section in Huyton library, and her staff have given valued assistance on many occasions. Dr John Willmott has given generously of his time and expertise; Miss D. Winterbotham, Lancashire County Library, provided kind advice whilst Mrs Yvonne Thompson, West Lancashire District Library, compiled the list of Bailey's published works. Miss Suzanne Yee, for some years a valued member of my staff, has prepared most of the illustrations from some very indifferent material and my son, Mark, of Gardner Systems plc., Liverpool, has provided oft-needed guidance in the mysteries of word-processing. Mr Keith Sergeant, Flexipress Printers, Ormskirk has personally supervised the actual production of the book. To them all I record my very sincere thanks.

The cost of the publication of the book has been borne by the Sponsors who are listed elsewhere between its covers. To have been thus relieved of all financial concern has greatly eased the task of production. The knowledge that the proceeds of the sale of the book will go directly to the benefit of the school surely brings the project to a satisfactory conclusion.

Aughton, 1993   *J. Sidney Bailie*

PART 1

The History of
PRESCOT GRAMMAR SCHOOL and PRESCOT SCHOOL

A HISTORY OF THE SCHOOL *Francis A. Bailey*

1 - THE EARLY YEARS

The will of Gilbert Lathum, Archdeacon of Man, dated 10th October, 1544, and discovered in the 1920's at Somerset House, contains, among its many bequests, the following:-

> " Item, I will a free gramer scole to be foundyt at Preskott, the master to haue yerely for his stypend vij Ii. . . . .
>
> Item, I will that in case a scholemaster can not be gotten to contynue for vii Ii. a yere, then the said vj Ii. (sic) to be given to thexhibicion of sixe poore scholers in Cambridge and Oxforde."

The precise meaning to be attached to the testator's words will be considered presently. First, we may sum up what we know - and it is unfortunately very little - about the testator himself.

Lathum's Parentage and Career.

Of Lathum's parentage, all that can be stated with certainty is that he belonged to one of the several branches of the family resident within the extensive parish of Prescot. In his lineage he was allied to the great Lancashire house of Stanley : in fact, it was by marriage with a Lathum heiress, a century and a half previously, that the Stanleys had first come into possession of their estates in this county. Of the relatives mentioned by Lathum in his will, the majority occur in the parish registers, court rolls and other records of Prescot and district. The provision of £20 "to be bestowed in Preskot parishe and Hyden (i.e. Huyton) parishe amonges my kynsfolke .... after their necessite and povertie", and another £20 "for a prest to singe at Preskot for my father and mother and me and my frendes, by the space of three yeres", is ample proof of his local origin.

Lathum was probably a protégé of the great educational benefactress, Margaret, Countess of Derby, better known as the Lady Margaret Beaufort, for he was associated with St. John's College, Cambridge, at the time of its foundation under the terms of her will. He graduated in or before 1513, received his master's degree in 1516, and became a bachelor of divinity in 1524. He appears to have held fellowships at both St. John's and Jesus Colleges, with other university appointments, at various times. Subsequently, he was Rector of Swanscombe, Kent, 1526-46, of Great Shelford, Cambs., to 1527, of Elton, Yorks.,

1533-46, and of Blore, Staffs. He was Master of St. Katharine's-by-the-Tower, 1536-46, and Archdeacon of Man from 1546 (or earlier) until his death in 1552. It will be noted that, like Wolsey and many other clerics of the period, he was a pluralist.

At the date of his will, Lathum was apparently in residence at the college of Stoke-by-Clare in Suffolk, for he provides for £5 to be " disposed for me the tyme of my buriall, yf I departe at Stoke College," namely, 2s. to the dean, 20d. each to the canons, 16d. each to the vicars choral, 12d. each to the clerks, 4d. each to the choristers, and the residue " to be distributed amonges poore people". It is of interest to observe in passing that the dean of the college then was Matthew Parker, the future archbishop. Before Lathum's death, the College had been dissolved, and we have no evidence of the actual place of burial.

Religious Changes.

In his later years, Lathum witnessed the first phases of that momentous event in our national life, the English Reformation. There is evidence that he did not view the religious changes with approval. The tenor of his will is indicative of his conservative outlook : he bequeathed "my best gilt cupp with the image of Jhesu on the cover" to the Princess Mary, subsequently queen, and as one of his executors he nominated Dr. Richard Smith, of Oxford University, a leading champion of the old system.

When Lathum died, in 1552, Edward VI was on the throne and the Reformers in power. Dr. Smith had fled abroad, the other executor refused to act, so administration of the will was granted to Edmund Lathum, next of kin. Shortly afterwards, however, on the accession of the Catholic Mary, Dr. Smith returned, and took over his duties as executor. "Myndinge to perfourme the said legacye and bequests", he "did delyver into thandes of one Thomas Eccleston of the said paryshe, esquyer, to thuse of the said parishioners, the summe of three skore poundes", in part payment of the £140 needed to provide the schoolmaster's stipend of £7 a year.

Chancery Action.

A remarkable development then ensued. The churchwardens of Prescot laid claim to the control of the money, and, in 1557, after the refusal of Mr. Eccleston to hand over the £60 in his possession, and of Dr. Smith to pay then, the £80 outstanding, they appealed to Sir Robert Rochester, Chancellor of the Duchy of Lancaster - not the last Chancery action in connection with the school funds. In the following year, before the case could be concluded, Mr. Eccleston died, and Dr. Smith again fled abroad, never to return, in consequence of the succession to the throne of the Protestant Elizabeth. It may be presumed that in these circumstances the churchwardens were awarded judgment.

For an understanding of what probably lay behind this episode, we must glance back at a second sequence of events, connected with the chantry gilds, or religious fraternities, of the parish. Three such gilds, named in honour of the Holy Cross, Our Lady and St. Catherine, existed at Prescot, each possessing a side altar in the parish church and employing its own chaplain for the singing of requiem masses. Such chantry priests were often schoolmasters also, but whether any regular school, supported by gild funds, existed here before 1546 is quite uncertain. A payment of 4d. "to Robert Webster, scoler, for his reward and labour" in helping to make the church candles, is recorded in the churchwardens' accounts of 1524-5. But whether the presence of this "scholar" may be held to presume the existence of a school is doubtful.

More conclusive, however, is the presentment by the jurors at Prescot court leet, on 10th June, 1547 : "we fynde ... that all the town hath stopped the watercourse and the kyngs strete afore the scholehowse". This is sufficient evidence of the existence of a school at Prescot before the death of Gilbert Lathum and before the dissolution of the chantries. This school may then have been long in existence, but there is some evidence, on the other hand, which points to a local decision, in 1545 or 1546, to forestall confiscation of the gild funds by converting them to educational uses. On this theory, the schoolhouse mentioned in 1547 would be of recent erection.

The Chantries Act was first passed in 1545, but had not been put into execution before the death of Henry VIII in 1547. A second Act was then passed, which resulted in the actual suppression of the chantries in 1548, their property being confiscated by the Crown. As early as 1546-7, the church-wardens' accounts reveal that Peter Eccleston, a churchwarden travelled to Chester "anendes Saynt Katheryns stocke" and in view of what transpired later it is permissible to infer that his mission was to try to save some at least of these funds for the maintenance of the school.

Lord Derby's Letter.

In 1549-50 the two churchwardens, Peter Eccleston and Robert Worsley "went to Lathum (Lord Derby's seat) to obteyne my lords letter for the forthering of the *free* scolle." The expression "free school" should be noted. If a "grammar

3

school" at Prescot already existed, it was presumably not a "free grammar school," that is, it did not teach "grammar" or Latin literature free of charge. It will be remembered that Gilbert Lathum's bequest was for "a free gramer scole to be foundyt," which may be interpreted as meaning either that a new school was to be founded, or that an existing school was to be provided with sufficient endowment to enable the master to dispense with fees for the teaching of "grammar." The object of the churchwardens' efforts in 1549-50 (this was before Lathum's death) was precisely similar, the founding of a free school, but, being probably unaware of Lathum's intended benefaction, they petitioned the King for the allocation of the confiscated chantry funds. Such a petition would ordinarily have had small prospect of success, unless it could be shown that the funds had been used for this purpose prior to the dissolution, but in this case the good offices of Lord Derby, one of the most influential nobles of his day, were instrumental in procuring an exceptional royal grant. (It is notable that the Chantry Commissioners' Reports, and the Schools' Continuance Warrants, make no mention of a school at Prescot ; nor is there any reference to the gild " stocks.") The facts are recorded in a manuscript of some forty years later as follows:-

" ARTICLES CONCERNINGE THE SCOOLE OF PRESCOTT, THE ERECTION AND CONTINUANCE THEROF.

1. That divers stockes or sommes of money within this parishe of Prescotte in tyme of superstitione, given and allotted to superstitious uses, as anniversaries, obits, trentalls, mayntenance of a prist and alter in such a chappell and suche like : and by the kinge of famous memorie Edw. 6 (whoe placinge in this realme sincere religione and abolishinge all superstitione) seysed into his handes amonghts others, the said stockes and sommes of money. Afterwardes by the then Chanceler of the Duchie of Lanc., by his letters missive, converted for the mayntenance of a scoolmaster to be resident within the towne of Prescott.

2. That accordinglie the said sommes weare imployed and a scoolmaister in Prescott mayntened by manie yeares past.

3. That seence the furst gratious dispositione of our late soueraigne lord kinge Edw. 6., dyvers well devoted have givene great sommes to the like use of mayntenance of a scoolmaister and scoole in Prescott.

4. That the inhabitants of the town of Prescott, by the space of manie yeares, payed of theire owne charges, schollmaster wages, to thend to encrease the stockes of the said scoole, as also the perpetuall continuance of the said scoole within the said towne.

4

5. Wheareas dyvers of the sommes of money apperteyninge unto the scoole
    bee now in the handes of divers tenants of divers lands which unwillinglie
    paie the same sommes, my lords letters in this behalf unto the landlords by
    name maye ether drawe the stockes or sommes of money forthe of theire
    handes, and then to be delivered to the well affected towardes the schoolle
    : or otherwise to bynd them with such sewerties as shalt be thought meete
    unto such as indevor the good of the said scoolle."

The latter part of this statement bears on the crisis which arose in
Elizabeth's reign, and which will be recounted presently. Among the "dyvers
well devoted" who gave "great sommes," Gilbert Lathum was presumably
included, since as we have seen his bequest was not procured until after the
Chancery suit of 1557.

The "Stocks".

That the funds of the three chantry gilds were in fact transferred to the
school can be proved from contemporary records. One instance may be cited,
though there are others. In 1546, the court roll mentions a cottage in Trap Lane
(now Garden Walk) yielding an annual rent of 4d. each to the Rood stock, Our
Lady stock and St. Catherine's stock. In the rental of Prescot manor, 1592, the
same cottage is recorded as yielding 12d. yearly to the school.

It will be noticed that the chantry funds were known as "stocks", and it is
of interest to recall that for centuries after, the old school endowment continued
to be known as the "stock". At the period under review it consisted mainly of
cattle, which were hired out to different persons for an annual charge of 12d. per
beast.

Having secured the chantry stocks for the school, the churchwardens were
soon threatened with the loss of them again, for an order of Queen Mary, c.
1556, addressed to Robery Brassey, vicar, and Thomas Eccleston and Thomas
Parr, esquires, enjoined that "certen stocks of kyen and other things be restored"
to the use and maynteyance of certain priests as in times past. How far this order
had been carried out before Mary's death in 1558 we cannot say. Very shortly
after it was issued, the churchwardens brought their Chancery suit against Thomas Eccleston and Dr. Smith for Gilbert Lathum's legacy. It is reasonable to
assume that the two events were related, and that the churchwardens applied for
the Lathum fund because the loss of the chantry stocks would have jeopardised
the existence of the free school. That Mr. Eccleston figured in both events may

5

be explained simply by his position as the leading personage in this side of the parish. His refusal, with Dr. Smith, to give up the Lathum money was possibly due to his having formed a project of establishing a school in Eccleston, which in point of situation would have been a more convenient centre for the other townships of "Prescot side," as the northern half of the parish was called. Such a project was, as we shall see, energetically pursued by Thomas Eccleston's successor.

The Schoolwardens.

The sixteenth century court rolls of Prescot contain many references to officers variously termed "wardens", "guardians", "feoffees" or "governors" of the school endowments. They appear mostly in actions for the recovery of sums owing to the school for the hire of cattle or rent of land. The first such action occurred in 1557, when Peter Stockley and Hamlet Ratchdale, *gardiani stipendii ad ludimagistrum debiti,* recovered 11s. from Richard Bellerby for the hire of one beast. We may infer from this that Bellerby owed for a period of 11 years, that is, from 1546, the year in which, as mentioned above, the gild "stocks" may have been originally allocated by local agreement to the use of the school. The schoolwardens may therefore be regarded as the successors of the gild wardens who appear in earlier court rolls on similar business.

In later times the schoolwardens were annually appointed at a parish meeting or vestry on St. Luke's Day (18th October), and this may have been the practice from the beginning. They were four in number, representing the "quarters" of "Prescot side", that is, one for Prescot, Whiston and Rainhill, one for Eccleston and Rainford, one for Windle and Parr, and one for Sutton.

2-THE ELIZABETHAN CRISIS.

The new crisis, which arose in the middle of Elizabeth's reign, was due fundamentally to the religious conflict, particularly bitter in this parish, where, as the Bishop of Chester stated in 1584, "the people are most obstynate and contemptuous." It was precipitated by the appointment as Vicar in 1583 of Thomas Mead, M.A., a zealous reformer, nominated by that prominent divine, Dr. Roger Goad, Provost of King's.

The Vicar Explains.

In a letter to the Provost, dated 26th May, 1586, the Vicar gave the following account of the situation:-

" Sir, we have a free schole in this towne of Prescote, whiche is no smale commoditie to the towne, and a greate furtherance for religion. Scholemasters and ministers ether do or shold ioyne hande in hande for instruction of youth, to teach them the trewe feare of God. Our gentlemen of this parishe wherof I am minister, perceavinge my indevor hearin, of late, within this fewe dayes, entered consultation to remove the schole ij miles from the churche, purposings hearby to hinder my good corse, which God be thanked hathe not beene without some profite ; my trust is greater will followe. I have withe some displeasure unto my selfe stayed it for this time. I beseche you (good sir) as you tender the good procedinge in religion, be erneste with my Lord of Darby, that it be not at anie time removed. The onlie reformation that we can hope for in this corrupte contrie is, that children be truly and diligently catechized, for I thinke that superstition is so grownded in the adged, that without the rare mercie of God deathe must parte it. I doubt not but God will blesse our labors conceringe the instruction of youthe, whiche wilbe better and withe greater ease performed wen the minister and the scholmaster are one hand at the elbow of the other, and therfore our forefathers, seeinge this, have founded ther free scholes not far from the mother churche. All our gentelmen are ether obstinate recusantes or verie cold professors, and wold gladly worke to hinder the good corse of the worde."

The matter, from the Vicar's point of view, could hardly be put more clearly. Resolved to replace " superstition " by sound doctrine, he looked upon the school as a most effective instrument for furthering his mission, thus arousing the resentment of the many influential parishioners who openly or covertly adhered to the old religion. These, equally alive to the importance for the future of controlling the education of the young, resolved to frustrate his design by moving the school out of the town. If, as is probable, the majority of the schoolwardens and the holders of the "stocks" were in favour of the removal, their plan became quite feasible and practicable, for, with the endowments in their control, they were in a position to transfer the school to any other suitable place within the parish. That the Vicar succeeded "with some displeasure" in "staying it for this time" (that is, for the time being) was, in the circumstances, a definite achievement. As will be seen, he was aided by the reluctance of the townspeople to see the school moved into the country. The possibility of an appeal to Lord Derby was also, no doubt, a factor which contributed to the result.

The Fourth Earl of Derby.

Henry Stanley, fourth Earl of Derby (1531-93), courtier, ambassador, Privy Councillor, Lord High Steward, Lord Lieutenant and Ecclesiastical Commissioner, was a personage of both national and local importance. His three chief residences, at Lathom, Knowsley and New Park, were all in close proximity to the parish of Prescot. He was the son of Edward, the third Earl (1509-72), who had, as previously noticed, used his influence "for the forthering of the free scolle" in 1549 or 1550.

Lord Derby stood also in a special relation to Prescot, for the Stanleys had long farmed the Rectory on very favourable terms from King's College. He was thus entitled to the corn tithes of the extensive parish, and to the manorial profits of the town of Prescot, of which he was the nominal Steward. His patronage was shown by his aid to the townsmen in asserting their claim to exemption from tolls in Liverpool market, by his giving them preference in the digging of peat in Knowsley Park, and by his allowing them to pasture their cattle there at half the rate charged to others. No one would have questioned Lord Derby's right to intervene in the dispute concerning the school, if he chose to do so. His reluctance to offend the local gentry was however such that, but for the exercise of pressure by Dr. Goad, he would in all probability not have so chosen.

That Goad did write as the Vicar requested, and that Lord Derby did take action, is proved by further references in letters by the Vicar in 1591-2, as follows:-

(Vicar to Provost, 6 June, 1591). "Our schole is greatly hindered by a gentelman in our parishe, Mr. Eccleston, and it had bene clene overthrowne but that my Lord made some stay therof, and yett is it greatly shaken, and it is like clene to decay except some good order be taken withe spede : and in my minde this wold further it marvolusly, if you wold direct a thankefull letter unto my Lord for that he hathe done, withe a request to continew his honorable favor and furtherance unto the schole."

(Vicar to Provost, 18 January, 1591-2). " Sir, as I remember, bothe by letter and private speche, I made you acquaynted withe our schole in Prescot towne, howe our gentlemen in the parishe, not well affected in religion, sought to remove it from the churche above ij miles . . . Once I

8

prevented ther purpose : another time I was a meanes to my Lord of Dar-
bie to stay it in the towne. As yett ther is such cuninge meanes wrought
that, excepte you direct a letter to my Lord *to continew his honorable
favorable favor,* it is like clene to be lost : and I knowe that at your request
he will stand ernest in the cause ... *I beseche you therefore that you wold
direct your letters unto my lord givinge him thanks for that, that alredie
he hathe done, withe a farther request fully to settell bothe schole and
stocke:* otherwise it will decay."

(Vicar to Lord Derby, c. 1592) . . . . . Therefore none so meete as your
honor, being now an highe commissioner in causes ecclesiasticall, to
ordeyne a place, to provide a scholmaster and to make lawes for a schole ;
whiche your good Lordshipe most honorably have provided for, when the
gentelmen of our parishe layed asid the care therof, appoyntinge that the
schole shold remayne in the same place, and have provided for the towne
scholmasters."

Lord Derby's Visits.

Lord Derby's intervention, referred to above, probably took place in
1587, for he paid two personal visits to the town on 23rd May and 16th June of
that year. On the latter occasion he presided at the annual court leet for the first
and, as it proved, the last time. The court roll makes incidental reference to an
obligation on the part of two tenants, Richard Rigby and James Atherton, to pay
£42 to Thomas Webster, schoolmaster, at the feast of Purification (2nd February) next following. This may be an echo of one of the decisions made at the previous visit. The effect of Lord Derby's intervention was, apparently, to secure a
further postponement for five years, as stated in another passage of the letter last
quoted:-

"When the gentlemen had a like intent before, a good while since, it was
then generallie concluded, that the schole shold remayne wher it is for the
benefite of the poore towne upon this condition, if the towne of Prescot
wold maynteyne (it) for the whole parishe of ther owne charges the space
of five years, that the common stockes might increase, for the greater
benefite of the sayd schole in the end and expiration of the sayde years,
whiche condition the poore towne of Prescot to ther greate charges have
performed : therefore it sholde now be agaynst all equitie, right and con-
science (to) have it taken from them."

It may be conjectured that the £42, allocated to the schoolmaster by the
court leet in 1587, was in lieu of stipend (at £7 a year) for six years, namely,
the arrears for the year since May, 1586, when the crisis first arose, and that

9

which would become due in the next five years, 1587-92.

The five years' postponement, during which the school was maintained by Prescot township, ostensibly to allow the "stocks " to increase, really perhaps because the bulk of the funds was withheld by the Vicar's opponents, was (if our surmise is correct) due to terminate in May, 1592. The Vicar's letters of 1591-2 thus appear to have been written when a renewal of the crisis became imminent.

Mr. Eccleston.

The Mr. Eccleston mentioned as the prime mover in the plan to transfer the school, was Henry Eccleston, of Eccleston Hall, esquire, son of the Thomas Eccleston who, with Dr. Smith, had withheld the Lathum bequest from the churchwardens in 1557. The Ecclestons long continued to be, in the main, a Roman Catholic family. Both father and son were actuated in all probability by the additional desire to establish a school within their own township of Eccleston. That the proposed new site "above ij miles" from the church, was in fact within the latter township may be deduced from the further developments in connexion with a school in Eccleston, to which reference will be made later.

The recurrence of the crisis in 1592 was one reason for the Provost's decision to come himself to Prescot. He presided at a stormy Court Leet on 26th May, where, according to his own notes still preserved at King's College, it was agreed, amongst other things, that the school should be settled at Prescot."

Meeting at Knowsley Hall.

Nearly a fortnight later, a meeting of "the parisshioners of Prescott" was convened by Lord Derby at Knowsley Hall. The Earl, the Provost, the Vicar and many gentry and others, including Mr. Eccleston, were present, and it was there agreed and finally decided

> "that from henceforthe the Grammar Schole shalbe, and be contynued kepte and taughte at and within the towne of Prescott, untill suche tyme as the said Erle or his heires, with a lyke consente of the gentlemen and parisshioners, shall see and conceyve speciall cause to remove it."

Orders were made for the compilation of a full account of the "stocks", with a list of persons in whose hands they then were; for the renewal of the necessary "bounds, billes and sureties", and the payment of all arrears owing, "as they will answeere the contrarie at theire perills"; that "a scholemaster shall immedyatlie be provided and begyn to teache schole at Prescott at the feaste of St. Michaell tharchaungell now nexte coming, and have thallowance and

10

exhibicion due for thexercysinge of that place" ; and that the existing schoolwardens be then "discharged, and others chosen to supplie theire steeds in suche sorte as heretofore they have bene, and that noe scholewardens shalbe contynued longer then for one whole yeare".

Original Site of the School.

After this, there was no longer any question of moving the school away from the town. If a school were wanted in Eccleston, it would have to be a new school, with a new endowment. The old school remained on its original site until 1759, when, as will be seen, it was removed to another part of the town. In the survey of the manor which Dr. Goad caused to be made in 1592, the site of the school can be quite definitely identified as that of the present General Post Office in Church Street. The actual words of the survey, translated from the Latin, are:-

"the Wardens of the Free School of the parish of Prescott, to be taught in Prescott, hold by copy, to the use of the said school, a certain building, late Plumton's, called *the schole house* , abutting E on a house belonging to the same school, W and S on the way, N on the lands of Robert Plumpton;

Also a burgage with a garden, in the tenure of Edward Scasbrick, abutting E on *the Schole house* W on the way to Lirpoole, S on the lane called *chirch yeard lane* , paying 4d. rent".

The words "late Plumton's" indicate that the land on which the school stood had formerly belonged either to George Plumpton (d. 1558) or to his son Robert, who in succession held the land adjacent. The significance of the words "to be taught in Prescott" will be apparent from the narrative just related.

Eccleston Grammar School.

The project of establishing a school in Eccleston was revived about ten years later, but on a different basis. A retired ecclesiastical judge, residing in Rainhill, James Kenwrick by name, was desirous of founding a free grammar school and chapel in Prescot parish, and was willing to assign a sum of £300, owed to him, as an endowment. Edward Eccleston, esquire, who succeeded his father Henry in 1598, induced Kenwrick to agree to the building of the school and chapel in Eccleston, by promising a further £100 and an acre of land by the king's highway near "Eccleston thorn" on the "middle hill". Shortly after making this agreement, Kenwrick died (1603), and the project thereafter remained in abeyance until 1684, when the old school building, now called Seddon's

Cottage, was erected on Eccleston Hill. In the meantime, as will be seen, Kenwrick's £300 had experienced some strange adventures.

There can be little doubt that the site of this later school on Eccleston Hill was actually the place "above ij miles" from the parish church, to which Henry Eccleston had designed to move Prescot Grammar School in 1586. Lancashire miles were, be it noted, long ones, as the rod, pole or perch of 8 yards (instead of 5½) was then in general use in these parts.

3-SCHOOL LIFE.

Is it possible to write a description of the School as it was in its early days? The answer to this question is a qualified negative. No actual view of the original school has been preserved, nor are there any records of its educational activities. The most we can do is to offer some observations based on our general knowledge of the type of school of which this is an example.

The Outward Scene.

The present G.P.O. in Church Street, which occupies the original site, affords reliable data as to the ground dimensions, although the building itself has doubtless undergone several reconstructions since its disuse as a school in 1759. The school was housed in one large schoolroom, upwards of 50 feet in length by 20 feet in breadth, capable of accommodating some sixty scholars. It might therefore be described as a school of average size. We have no record of the number of boys actually in attendance.

The master sat on a raised arm-chair at one end, and his assistant or usher, if he had one, sat at the other. The boys occupied benches ("forms") ranged in rows along the two long sides, leaving a broad space in the middle. They were grouped according to age and attainment, the "upper forms" being on the master's right. The master, in his university gown, and having his indispensable birch-rod in his hand or within easy reach, called the different " forms " before him in turn.

Classical Curriculum.

The school existed essentially for the teaching of Latin, then regarded as the universal language of scholarship. Education began, continued and ended with the classics. Save in the lowest forms, all use of English in school, and sometimes even in the playground, was forbidden. Every boy provided his own pen, ink, paper and textbooks, while the school had its own small library of chained dictionaries and other reference books. The standard grammar, which provided the groundwork of education, was for centuries that known as Lily's or the Eton Latin Grammar. The pupils soon passed on to more advanced studies in prose and verse composition and in the texts of Latin authors both ancient and "modern". The upper "forms" proceeded to the study of Greek, and even Hebrew.

Boys entered school usually at the age of seven or eight (sometimes earlier), in order to be ready for the university at fifteen or sixteen. They were expected to be able to read and write in English before admission, so that instruction in "grammar" might begin at once. Much of the supervision, in and out of school, was delegated to the abler scholars as "monitors" or prefects. School hours were commonly from 6 to 11 a.m. and 1 to 6 p.m. in summer, and 7 to 11 a.m. and 1 to 5 p.m. in winter, with fifteen-minute recesses at about 9 a.m. and 3 p.m. There was a half-holiday each week, usually on Thursday, and vacations at Christmas, Easter, Whitsuntide and (in some cases) Michaelmas. Saints' days and other holy days were usually holidays, after compulsory attendance at church in the morning, and there was no school on the fair day. There were no organised games, as time spent in play was then commonly regarded, by grown-ups at least, as time wasted.

School discipline, and the general standard of teaching, were dependent, then as now, on the capability and conscientiousness of the individual master. There was much corporal punishment, the result not only of an exacting curriculum but also of a general acceptance of the biblical precept "spare the rod and spoil the child". The boys had, however, their own privileged occasions, as at the annual "potation" provided by the master, the Shrove Tuesday cock-fighting, and the Christmas " barring out."

Adam Martindale's Experiences.

Some very interesting sidelights on the old grammar schools of our district, in the sixteen-thirties, occur in the autobiography of the Puritan preacher Adam Martindale, who was born at Moss Bank near St. Helens in 1623. Though the schools at St. Helens and Rainford, which he mentions, were probably inferior to Prescot, he succeeded in obtaining a remarkably good classical education. Being himself rather a paragon as a scholar, he writes very critically of some of his teachers. The following extracts illustrate well the good and bad features of such schools:-

"About the middle of January, 1630, when schooles began to be revived after Christmasse, I was sent to the free schoole of St. Hellens, almost two miles from my father's house, a great way for a little fat short legged lad (as I was) to travell twice a day ....."

"My first master was a young ingenious sparke, having a good full schoole, but so bad an husbande (i.e., manager) that he quickely spoiled all and left us. A worse followed him, viz., an old humdrum curate, that had almost no scholars, nor deserved any, for he was both a simpleton and a tipler. He and I parted when I was learning mine accidence without booke. The third I went too was a woman (daughter to a famous schoolemaster) that had some smattering of Latin ... so that with her I did something better than quite loose my time, but not much."

"Next I was placed under another schoolemaster at St. Hellens Chappell, who was brought up at the then famous schoole of Winwicke, whence multitudes were almost yearely sent to the University. This master ... was scholar sufficient for me then ; but he was a very silly and inconstant man, always making new laws, in-so-much that if a boy had beene absent a day or two, he knew not how to behave himself for feare of transgressing some new ridiculous order or other. Nor was this the worst, but being a married man with a charge, and very poore, he lay open to impressions from such as could fee him well, to carrie partiality amongst his scholars. One of these acts ... (when two 'errant dunces,' one a ' gentleman,' the other well-to-do, were set above him and kept there in spite of his winning the right to the place) ... occasioned my leaving him."

"My father ... removed me to Raineford, a schoole somewhat nearer then St. Hellens, but more costly, because no free schoole as the other was. But the cost was prettie well bestowed, for though the master was brought up at the same schoole with the former, he was a man of farre better parts, both natural and acquired ; diligent enough in looking to us, not onelie as to grammar-learning, but as to our profitting in the catecheticall grounds of religion ... His worst fault while he stayed there was that he was humourous (i.e., capricious) and passionate, and sometimes in these moods he would whip boys most unmercifully for small or no faults at all . . ."

"He afterwards succeeded my former master at St. Hellens, whither I followed him... (He gives details of his studies in Latin and Greek.)..... All that were presumed by their standing able to discourse in Latin were tinder a penalty if they either spoke English or broke Priscian's head (i.e., rules of grammar) ; but barbarous language (i.e., "dog Latin"), if not

14

incongruous for grammar, had no punishing but derision. These were the orders we were subject to at teaching houres . . . and sometimes (when the humour took him) he would tie us to them at our times for play. (The master's 'humours' grew worse until at last 'there was no abiding with him'.)"

A perfect master at last.

"... In the interim, there was a newe schoolemaster come to the old footing-place at Rainford that had the name of a very civill man, and a good teacher ; and that not without cause . . . It was no small prejudice to me, that the popish gentrie in the neighbourhood were so fond of him; yet I believe he was, and still is (if alive) a protestant ... Whatever was his (religious) opinion, he was an eminently able and diligent master. He had beene brought up, not onely at a good schoole in Bolton, but after at the University a good season (I have heard five yeares) where having a great affection to the Greeke tongue, an opportunity to heare the public professor, and to converse with other men, he had attained to a marvellouse exactnesse in pronouncing it in the University-manner, which till then I had not heard of. He was also skillfull in the derivations of words, teaching us many that we could not find in any lexicon."

"Nor was he sleight in examining us about the dialects, not onely in poets, but even in the Greek Testament ; wherein he made us to observe the Hebraismes, Latinismes, and idiomes. I heard once a confident scholar say the Greeke Testament is perfectly free and cleane from all dialects ; but it is a great mistake, as our master would have told him."

"He taught us also to make Greeke exercises, in prose and verse ; and both in these, and what we made in Latine, he expected not only congruity but elegancie. He spake very good Latine to us in a constant way; put us to take outour lessons ourselves, and, in examining them he stood not so much upon parsing (as they called it) or scanning of verses and proving them, to which he found us well inured, as upon rhetorical tropes and figures . . . He was also very notable at teaching us to observe all allusions in profane authours to the Sacred Scriptures, insomuch that anything leaning that way should hardly passe his observation ... To conclude, he seemed to be a man made for a schoolemaster, and was most excellent to give the finishing stroak to a countrey scholar."

"He also removed to St. Hellens, and was the onely schoolemaster that within the time of my observation went away thence a sober man. I followed him thither, and remained his scholar betwixt two and three yeares, in which time he tooke a great deale of paines with me, especially in Homer's Odysses. And about the beginning of July, 1639, being above sixteene yeares of age, I tooke my solemne leave of him and my schoole fellowes, being allowed by him as readie for the University."

Preferences at Brasenose.

Unfortunately, Martindale was prevented by the disorders of the times from pursuing a University career. It is presumable that he would have gone to Brasenose College, Oxford, the favoured resort of Lancashire and Cheshire students since its foundation in 1509 by William Smith, Bishop of Lincoln, a native of Cuerdley in Prescot parish, and Sir Richard Sutton, of Sutton, in Cheshire. The founders stipulated that preference to the College fellowships should be given to natives of Lancashire and Cheshire, especially to those of the parishes of Prescot and Prestbury. Among the early benefactors of the college was Humphrey Ogle, Archdeacon of Hereford, a native of Whiston, who provided for two scholarships from Prescot parish. There can be no doubt that these scholarships and preferences added to the prestige of the old grammar schools of this parish, which numbered at least four, those of Prescot, Farnworth, St. Helens and Rainford. In the case of our own school, these benefits were, as we shall see, maintained in force until within the last hundred years.

4-THE SCHOOLWARDENS' ACCOUNTS.

Although records of its educational activities are almost non-existent, there is no lack of evidence to prove the continuity of the school's existence through the ages. This evidence is mainly concerned with the financial side. Two of the sources are of particular value, namely, the original Schoolwardens' accounts of the years 1678-88, discovered ten years ago in the Parish Church Vestry, and an abstract, made in 1755, and recently discovered in the offices of Mr. W. A. Cross, of an old "School Book", beginning in 1610.

The Stocks "decayed"

There can be no doubt that, as a result of the Elizabethan crisis, the finances of the school had remained seriously embarrassed. In a letter of about 1609, the Vicar (Mr. Mead), writing to Mr. Orme, a commissioner of Lord Derby, says : " I pray you lett me have execution granted presently (i.e., immediately) agaynst Thomas Garrard for the schoole stockes : if it weare not for the schoole I wold not be so erneste." It is evident that the old " stocks " or

16

endowments had not all been recovered after the Elizabethan crisis, despite the Knowsley decree of 1592. The Thomas Garrard here named may be identified with one of the leading gentry, Thomas Gerard, of Bryn, Esq. (created baronet in 1611) who as lord of the manor of Windle and a property-holder in Prescot town was of much local importance.

At Christmas, 1614, the school stocks numbered 246, each being worth 10s. Of these, 149 were "old" (presumably going back to before 1592) and 97 "new". Of the 149 "old stocks", however, 64 were "decayed" (i.e., not recovered), so the value of the "old stocks" had actually dwindled to £44 10s., a mere fraction of the original endowments. The "new stocks" were the result of a serious effort to restore the finances, and were raised by a variety of means.

First, about 40 stocks were given by particular donors, King's College and Thomas Eccleston, of Parr, gent., each giving 10, Laurence Webster, of Prescot, and " Robert Garnet's uncle, of Whiston," giving 4, others (including "Widow Glover") 2, others (including "Widow Dichfield at the Cock-pit House" and "James Taylor's mother-in-law") 1, whilst Thomas Halsall and "the gentlemen present at taking the school account", each contributed half a stock. Thomas Lancaster, of Rainhill, Esq., who died in 1696, bequeathed 9 stocks to the school, and also £10 to the poor " out of which the Vicar reserved £3 to the school for bringing up poor children, thus increasing the number to 15.

The Vicar, too, was instrumental in getting the "New Year's gift" (a special collection in church, usually used for church expenses) allocated to the school, 13 stocks being raised in 1610, 1611 and 1612 from this source. Fines or "pecuniary mulcts" imposed on parishioners by the Bishop's court at Chester, for ecclesiastical offences, were also allocated, as were the special charges made for the burial of recusants. In 1605, 8s. had been " gathered for Farnworth in the time of the plague there, for which there was no need, so the Vicar made it up " to 10s. for a school stock.

School Rents.

In addition to the interest on the stocks, the school had been accumulating a considerable revenue from rents on houses and land. The "old rents" before 1592 had amounted only to some five or six shillings a year, but between that date and 1609 there were notable additions., Mrs. Catherine Glover (" Widow Glover ") of Rainhill (d. 1611) assigned to the school in or about 1602 a rent charge of 10s. a year on several cottages in Eccleston Street, Prescot. Richard Harden, or Harwarden, of Whiston (d. 1600) by his will devised to the school a close called Barton's Hey in Cumber Lane in that township, which yielded an annual rent of 6s. 8d. Robert Conney, of Prescot, gent. (d. 1600) assigned a rent charge of 2s. on an acre of land in Rainhill.

Rents payable to the school were also charged upon all buildings newly erected on the waste land of the manor of Prescot. The Vicar's letter of 1609 refers to five such buildings, one of them "the play house builded uppon the wast by Mr. Richard Harrington", another " Mr. Malbon his horse mill, with rents varying from 12d. to 5s. This arrangement, which is perhaps unique, could only have originated with the consent of the lord of the manor (King's College) and the steward (Lord Derby), and it is therefore probable that it was made on the occasion of the meeting at Knowsley in 1592. That it was recognised as late as 1624 is shown by the following extract from the court roll of that year:-

> "Henry Prescott hath encroached a parcell of the wast in the fall lane, and theirupon hath built a cottage, the which Mr. Steward hath beene pleased to allow, theirefore for rentinge theirof, as hath beene heire used in such cases, we assesse him to pay yearely to the lord ijd. and to the schoole ijs. at the day usuall by equall porcions."

It is apparent from the following order, in the same court roll, that obligations of this sort were apt to be ignored:

> "Wheareas dyvers schoole tenements are enjoyed by dyvers severall persons in this towne, and such rents as are due both to the lord and the schoole are for the same in arere and unpaid, wee order that all such rents as are unpaid unto the lord from any such shalbe paid unto his baliffe, and all such rents as are due to the schoole shalbe paid to the schoole wardens, before the xxth of June next, otherwyse that the schoolewardens shall pay_ to the lord all such rent as is due to him, and then enter upon the posession of the severall tenements to the use of the schoole. And further that all such as hold the schoole tenements shall henceforth pay theire rents to the wardens at theire dayes and tymes when as the same shall become payable, upon payne to be middiately . . . put out of the possession of the said tenements as affouresaid."

It was one thing to make an order of this sort, and another thing to enforce it. The schoolwardens held office only for a year (although, despite the order of 1592, they were often re-appointed), and were unremunerated. It is likely enough that in many cases they were careless of their responsibilities and disinclined to undertake unpleasant duties. Certain it is that a number of such rents remained unpaid for long periods and were forgotten.

A temporary " windfall."

The schoolwardens' prime responsibility was in respect of the stocks, which constituted the great bulk of the endowments. Each warden collected the profits from the particular quarter of Prescot side for which he served. The stocks were so invested as to yield interest at the rate of 6 per cent. In 1653, for example, the rents amounted to £3/2/11, and the interest of the stocks, which had a capital value of £416/5/0, to £24/19/5. The great increase in the stocks since 1615 may be noted : it was due mainly to a fortuitous " windfall," and unfortunately, as will be seen, it was short-lived.

The wardens had frequently to sue in the manor court for sums owing, sometimes without effect. In 1602, for instance, Edward Stockley, schoolwarden, impleaded Mary Parker, widow, for a debt of £10. In 1616 the executor of "the late Edward Stockley, one of the schoolwardens", impleaded the same lady, the debt by this time having increased to £22. In 1626 Mrs. Parker - she had been a widow now, by the way, since 1595 - was again sued for the £22, and others owing sums to the school amounting to f40 were also proceeded against in this year.

The Kenwrick Fund.

The " windfall " mentioned above came as a sequel to the project for the erection of a school in Eccleston. As previously stated, a sum of £300 was assigned by James Kenwrick for the endowment of a school in the parish, and Edward Eccleston, Esq., offered £100 and an acre of land for the erection of it in Eccleston. Subsequently, Mr. Eccleston, who had been a recusant, decided to conform, and he then seems to have abandoned the project, as the religious motive which had actuated him was no longer operative. For many years Kenwrick's £300 remained in suspense, as it were, until in 1626, on the initiative of the Vicar and schoolwardens of Prescot, an inquiry was held before the Bishop of Chester, at Wigan. Henry Eccleston, Esq., who had succeeded his father, Edward, in 1624, appeared and declared himself "content the said schoole should be erected in Prescott". The other parties concerned were not so complaisant, and a year later, on 2nd October, 1627, the Bishop issued a decree ordering "that the schoole wardens of Prescott aforesaid do prosecute suites for obtaineinge the said 300 li".

The Fund gained-

For reasons partly politic and partly financial, the matter was deferred until 1641, when at parish meeting it was decided "that the school wardens should take about 50 li. which bas been collected for military services, to be employed against Mr. Kenwright for recovery of 300 Ii. chargeable upon his lands by Mr. James Kenwrick his uncle's will, and given to the free school of Prescott." The £50 "for military services" had been levied upon papists towards financing the abortive Scottish war of 1640, and it was doubtless with a sense of poetic justice that the money was appropriated to this other use.

It was not until 1650 that the question was settled in favour of the Prescot schoolwardens by a decree of the Commonwealth Court of Chancery. The money in dispute had, as we have seen, been actually procured by 1653. In January, 1654/5, a parish meeting decided, very commendably, to make a grant of £20 " to the wardens of the free school of St. Ellin " and another of £10 "to the wardens of the school of Rainford", whilst allotting what seems a very meagre sum of £18/16/0 "towards building the new school house at the free school of Prescot".

-and lost.

A sad blow was, however, soon to fall. Under the new political regime after the Restoration of 1660, the "papists" again raised their heads, the Eccleston family reverted to the old faith, the project of an Eccleston school was revived, and the decree of 1650 was reversed. A new Chancery decree of 14th July, 1669, ordered that £218/16/3 "received by certain persons as schoolwardens" be paid over to Thomas Malbon and James Gleast on behalf of the township of Eccleston. The Prescot wardens contested the case, employing a Prescot attorney, William Blundell, but after incurring legal charges totalling some £120, they were finally ordered, on 25th March, 1673, to pay £276/2/11, the increase being probably due to interest charges.

The original schoolwardens' accounts of 1678-88 therefore reveal the school in the throes of a new financial crisis. We learn that in 1674 the remaining stocks had been worth only £52/8/9. The school was without a master from March, 1673 to Michaelmas, 1674, thus affording a saving of £9/1/0 in interest and rent, which was added to capital. Mr. Brierley, appointed master in 1674, stayed only four years, during which he himself collected what rent and interest he could, to the amount of £28/14//5. This, the wardens contended, was £2/7/2 in excess of what was due to him, but Brierley claimed that £2 was "for the learninge of Edw. Blundell", the attorney's son, and this, after the latter's death in

1680, was recovered from his widow, along with other sums he was alleged to owe to the school.

New financial crisis.

Every effort was in fact now made to economise, and to search out old sources of revenue which had been allowed to lapse, including "severall rents mencioned in ould schoole booke of acct.," which "have not bin payd for xx years past or upward". A perpetual lease of the old schoolmaster's house for 10s. a year had been made by former wardens, although "the same is better than xxs. per annum ... and we conceive no wardens have such power, therefore desyre it may be considered". The following are among other details noted:

"Thomas Parr payd xl years together, as appears in ould books and how lost we know not. *(Added :)* 1688, recouvered.

We fund for neer xx years together Kings College to have payd by the hand of the vicar xs. per annum to the schoole master of Prescott, and how lost we know not, but desyre they may be moved therein.

Further, that one way of advance of schoole stockes was by the colleccions made att the Communion, as also by the beginge all pecuniary mulcts. The former is in power of vicar and wardens, and may be done, the other endeavoured."

Communion collections is apparently an interpretation of the earlier expression " New Year's gift." From the accounts of the next year, 1688, we learn that the Vicar and Churchwardens had consented to this appropriation, for the stocks were augmented by £2/8/8, " beinge moneys given att communions. The vicar, Edward Goodall, was himself at this time a schoolwarden, along with three other prominent parishioners, Edward Ogle, Daniel Lawton and Henry Lathom. By 1688, when the accounts terminate, the stocks had risen to £70, and the annual rents to about £3/15/0, thus affording the schoolmaster his yearly stipend of £7. This, curiously enough, is the same amount as the stipend specified by Gilbert Lathum in 1544, although the value of money had altered greatly in the meantime, and what might have been an adequate stipend in 1544 was certainly not so in 1688. But we must not imagine that the schoolmaster, at either of these dates, was wholly dependent on this meagre allowance. The reference to Edward Blundell is proof that, although the teaching was "free" to the poorer scholars, those parents who had the means to pay were expected to do so.

5-THE REMOVAL TO HIGH STREET.

The next seventy years of the school's history (1688-1758) were, as far as we can tell, comparatively uneventful. The process of recovery went on very satisfactorily for a time, aided by a series of generous benefactions, of which the first, and best, was a rent charge of £2 yearly on the Mill Hill House in Prescot, given in 1690 by Thomas Glover, of London, merchant. Other gifts, totalling £75, were made between 1690 and 1725, thus more than doubling the stocks. A portion of the new capital was used in 1697 for the purchase of the premises known at different times as the School End House, the Birch Tree and the Ring of Bells.

After several brief masterships, the school enjoyed for thirty seven years (1688-1725) the rule of Mr. Henry Waring, brother of "parson Waring", the schoolmaster of Great Crosby, doubtless with very beneficial results upon its work. Nicholas Fazakerley, the celebrated lawyer and politician, who was born at Prescot in 1682, doubtless received his schooling under Mr. Waring.

The master's stipend had by 1719 been increased to £10/10/- a year. On Waring's death, the Rev. Robert Chapman held the mastership for eighteen years (1731-49), and a grant of £40 was made (1731) for enlarging the schoolmaster's house at the west end of the school, "he to be at any further charge that may be necessary".

In 1732, the Vicar, Mr. Gwyn (a schoolwarden) proposed to King's College that the school stocks be used to erect a "shambles" on the waste for the butchers, the profits to be used for the benefit of the school, but we hear no more of the scheme.

An interesting benefaction, first mentioned in 1754, was the late Mr. Marsh's gift of 10s. a year for books for the use of Prescott School." These would doubtless be exercise books, then known as copy-books.

Changing conditions.

The school had now survived the first 200 years of its existence, during which the population of the town had increased from under 500 to about 2,500. There was a growing feeling that the old school, both as to its accommodation and its curriculum, was no longer adequate. Accordingly, a policy was adopted, probably on the initiative of Mr. John Chorley, Overseer of the Charities, of subsidising the school from the general charity funds of the town, and utilising it to meet the need for primary as well as more advanced education. At a meeting of the trustees of Mrs. Ellen Siddall's charity in 1754, it was decided to grant the

22

proceeds of the charity (then £9 a year) to Mr. John Robinson "the present teacher or instructor of poor children at the Grammar School within Prescott ... in order to teach such poor children belonging to Prescott aforesaid to read and write as the said trustees shall appoint from time to time, not exceeding eight in number", unless increases in the income justified the number being raised.

This new policy was greatly developed in the following years, and it had far-reaching results on the character of the school. First, it caused the "freedom" of the school, which had in theory been available to the whole of "Prescot side" of the parish, to become virtually restricted to Prescot township. Secondly, it tended to transfer the control of the school to the Court Leet and the charity trustees, with the result that the schoolwardens were gradually divested of their authority. Thirdly, it created what was in effect a separate department of the school, to become known in course of time as the "Lower Grammar School". Fourthly, it was the immediate cause of the transfer to a new schoolhouse on the Moss at the " back o' th' town."

Rebuilding Scheme.

After years of hesitation the Court Leet decided to sponsor the rebuilding scheme in 1759, and an appeal for public subscriptions was launched. It opened with a statement that at the last court (15th June, 1759):-

> "the Steward, the Homage, the principal officers and we the Foremen (i.e., Four Men), together with the chief part of the Copyholders their present, or afterwards made privy thereto, were unanimously of opinion that a new Gramer School was needfull and greatly wanted in this manor for the encouragement of learning and for the accomodation of the inhabitants of this town and neighbourhood."

The list of subscriptions, which was opened at the same court, is prefaced by the following:-

> "15th June, 1759. It being represented to us whose names are hereunto subscribed that the situation of the old Gramar School in Prescott is not only dangerously situated for the boys who are taught there, by reason of the narrowness of the street opposite thereto, and the many wheel carriages passing therein, but by farr too small in its dimensions to afford convenient room for the boys which may reasonably be expected to use the said school . . ."

A new site.

The narrowness of Church Street, which then formed part of the highway between Liverpool and London, is thus seen to have been the main reason for the change of site. There was no intention whatever of suppressing one school and founding another, for the above appeal expressly states that the contributions are to be paid to the Rev. Augustin Gwyn, vicar and schoolwarden, for erecting the new building "in such place and of such dimensions as he, the said Mr. Gwyn, and other the wardens of the said school, shall think most suitable."

The total amount subscribed was £94/13/5. A list of subscribers (not quite complete) contains 60 names, the largest donation being £10 from the celebrated lawyer, Nicholas Fazakerley, M.P., to whom allusion has been made above. The next largest sum was £5/5/0 from the Earl of Derby, the Rev. William Johnson, vicar of Whalley (who appears to have resided at Prescot), John Atherton, John Chorley, John Case and Henry Makin. The new building actually cost £154/18/5, the balance of £60 being advanced out of "Mr. Marrow's money" and other charity funds, in consideration of which, and of his being allowed the use of the old school, the master agreed to take two additional free pupils nominated by the charity trustees.

Mr. Eceleston's grant.

The site of the new school,, which lay within the bounds of the manor of Eccleston, was granted by Basil Thomas Eccleston, Esq., in the following terms:-

> "Forasmuch as the present wardens of the Grammar School of Prescott have applied to me for my consent, that they may use twenty yards square or four hundred superficial yards of the south side of Hackley Moss in the township of Eccleston and parish of Prescot and county of Lancaster, for the purpose of building a new school thereon and for appurtenances thereto,
>
> These are therefore to signify, that I do hereby grant them their said request under the annual payment of two pence to me and my successors, lords of the manor of Eccleston."

By his generosity on this occasion Mr. Eccleston may be said to have atoned in some degree for the misdeeds of his predecessors. Himself originally a Scarisbrick, he had adopted the name of Eccleston on succeeding to the estates, and was a Protestant.

The new school was completed in 1760 and, with later extensions, continued to serve its purpose till 1924, when the present buildings in St. Helens Road were opened. (The building is now used by the Lancashire Education Committee as a schools' clinic). The Rev. Abraham Ashcroft was master of the school from before 1759 until his death in 1785. He was assisted by Mr. William Houghton, c. 1759-95, described in the list of subscribers (1759) as "usher" and in the parish register as "schoolmaster". Other "schoolmasters" are mentioned in the parish register as being "of Prescot" in this period, but no evidence exists to connect them with this school, and a Court Leet memorandum of c. 1793 reveals that poor children were sent free not only to the Grammar School but also to "the Alms House School", which probably took the less promising of them. That a standard of proficiency was expected for admission to the Grammar School is shown by an order of the court in 1768:-

> "that no poor boy shall be admitted to be taught to read or write at the Gramar School in Prescott by and out of the Charities belonging to this town, untill they can read tollerably well and be recomended and approved ... by the trustees ... or a majority of them."

Conditions of scholarships.

More elaborate provisions were passed by the court in 1769, entitled "Rules to be observed with respect to the thirty scholars taught at Prescott school by and out of the Charities belonging to the township of Prescott". They may be summarised very briefly thus:-

1. The poorest boys, if suitable, to have preference.
2. The boys to be approved at an annual public meeting of copyholders and recommended to the Treasurer of the Charities, who will give them signed tickets and pay the "quarterage" amounting to 20s. a year.
3. No boy so ticketed is to be accepted by the schoolmaster if unsuitable ; nor is he to be taught after the end of the year unless supplied with a new ticket on beginning school after Christmas.
4. A notice of vacancies is to be put on the south wall of the school and on the town hall door by the master, and proclaimed by "the bell man".
5. Boys absent for a month without good reason to lose their places.
6. Each boy to produce a specimen of his writing four times a year, to be shown at stated meetings of the court, on pain of losing his place.
7. At least 10 of the 30 boys are to be "instructed in figures and accounts as well as in writing".

8. These rules do not indicate that the Charities are "annexed" to this particular school.

A list of the "free scholars" in this year (1769) has been preserved among Mr. W. A. Cross's manuscripts.

Teaching of girls.

In the private account-book of George Case, of Prescot (later Mayor of Liverpool, 1781) the following item appears for 31st August, 1765 : "Paid Mr. Ashcroft in full for my sister's schooling, 10s." This indicates that Mr. Ashcroft did not restrict his pupils to boys. It is likely however that Margaret Case was a private pupil taking lessons at the master's house. The need to make some provision for teaching girls led to the erection, in or before 1786, of a "new addition to the New School called the Girls' Room", in consideration of which the master agreed to teach one extra poor boy without payment. The "free scholars" were apparently all boys, and the Girls' Room was presumably for a class of fee-payers.

The number of "free scholars" in 1793 was 37. The master received £34 yearly for their instruction, three boys being taught gratis on account of the old school and the Girls' Room. In this year, Mr. John Wyke's legacy of £100 for the instruction of poor children "of Prescot parish" in the English tongue, writing, arethmatic, mathematics and particularly mechanicks," was applied to the teaching of four more "free scholars" at "the public school of Prescott", i.e., the Grammar School. The Rev. William Ellam, schoolmaster in 1803, received £39 for the " tuition " of 41 boys, together with £2/7/9 " for old school stock." About 500 copybooks were provided annually at a cost of 2/6 a dozen. The master's salary was increased in 1806 to £54/2/9, again in 1809 to £90, of which £8/19/0 consisted of school rents which he himself collected, and again in 1816, as the result of a legacy of £200 by the late Vicar, the Rev. Samuel Sewell.

It must be emphasised that the foregoing particulars relate merely to the primary department or "lower school", and that the "upper school" or Grammar School proper continued to exist and, doubtless, to flourish. Evidence of this will now be given.

6 - A CENTURY AGO.

Many references to the school occur in the account-book of Mr. John Jackson, Treasurer of the Prescot Charities, 1803-28. The expenditure in 1808 included £4/16 "paid Mr. Bates, for a Dinner, etc. for the Candidates, etc., on the appointment of New Master at the School", £2/2 "paid Mr. Lloyd for Examining the Candidates", £1/5/6 "paid for Advertising Vacancy in Prescot School, £1/4/9 "paid Mr. Thompson, for getting Advertised in the *Cumberland Packet* , the want of a Master at the Grammar School", and 1s. "paid for Cleaning the School".

The pains taken to provide a suitable schoolmaster, and the difficulty of finding one, are both evident, for the appointment was given to Mr. Timothy Redhead, who had apparently held the post before, for a short time, after the death of the Rev. Abraham Ashcroft, in 1785. In November, 1809, £1/4 was "paid Mr. Chorley for Advertising Master Wanted for Grammar School, Lancaster Paper", but this was probably an outstanding debt from the previous year. Mr. Redhead resigned in 1813, and was called upon to pay £1/15/6 "for Broken Windows at the School and School House", a fact which suggests that he was held responsible for this damage, perhaps the work of his private pupils, although a bill of 18/5 "towards repairing the Windows at the School" was also met by the Treasurer of the Sunday School.

Boarding School.

That Mr. Redhead had catered for boarders is shown by the following advertisement in the *Liverpool Post* and *Commercial Advertiser* early in 1809:-

"GRAMMAR SCHOOL, PRESCOT.

Mr. Redhead respectfully apprises the Public, that the business of the above School recommences on the 23d. instant, for the instruction of Young Gentlemen in Classical or Commercial Education.

Mr. R. flatters himself, from a limited number of Pupils, and their improvement, liberal treatment, and morals, being primary objects of his care, that the very agreeable and salubrious situation of Prescot, with such variety of eligible modes of conveyance to every part of the country, will merit the attention of Parents and Guardians.

Terms - Thirty Guineas per Annum.

Applications addressed as above will be duly attended to - Further particulars specified, and references, if required.

Prescot, 4th January, 1809."

Mr. Redhead had doubtless set himself out to attract pupils from Liverpool, where educational facilities were then woefully inadequate. The ancient Liverpool Grammar School, founded in 1515, was, in fact, discontinued in or about 1808, and Nicholas Carlisle in his Endowed Schools (1818) states that "several of the most respectable merchants in Liverpool" had received their education at Prescot Grammar School. It is evident that in the later eighteenth century, if not earlier, the school had enjoyed more than a merely local reputation, and that its activities were far from being confined to the teaching of reading, writing and (perhaps) arithmetic to the Prescot "free scholars".

The Classics.

Mr. Redhead was succeeded in 1813 by Mr. John Hamnett, who held the mastership until his death in 1849. Mr. Jackson's accounts for 1813 include £8/14 for "Expenses on Advertising in several Newspapers for a Master for the School , £1 paid Mr. Swale for Examining the candidates for the Grammar School in the Mathematicks," and £3/3 "paid Mr. Boardman, for Examining the Candidates in the Classics". This insistence upon adequate qualifications for teaching advanced subjects is notable evidence of the recognised status of the school. That the Classics were actually taught is shown by Carlisle's valuable account of the school in 1818, the latter part of which runs as follows:-

> "No statutes prevail beyond the election of a Master belonging to the Established Church and the instruction of the poor boys in the Church Catechism. The (free) boys are to be selected from the inhabitants of Prescot and consequently are nominated by the Steward and Officers of the Manor Court of Prescot.
>
> Boys from the School, if born in the parish, are sent to Brazen-nose College in Oxford, where they have a preference to seven Fellowships. Lancashire men also have the preference to several good exhibitions in the same College.
>
> The number of boys upon the foundation is now thirty-three. Three have been added in consequence of Mr. Sewell's legacy, but the admission of these was optional with the Master. There are no data by which the determinations of the Trustees are regulated beyond occasional usage, in the number of free boys.
>
> The number of day scholars is now also about thirty. It was formerly much greater, but owing to very gross mismanagement during the Mastership of the present gentleman's predecessor, who, soon after his appointment, rendered himself independent of the Trustees by procuring a licence to the school from the Bishop, and the consequent establishment of other schools in the town, it is probable that the number will not much increase.
>
> It must also be added that the town is poor, and that the terms for

instruction in the other schools are lower than in this. It is expected that the (free) boys at the time of admission should be able to read in a class (reader). They are admitted at the age of eight and at fourteen are superannuated, but these are points not scrupulously adhered to. The education of the free boys is confined to reading, writing and arithmetic.

The selection of books is left to the Master. The Eton Latin and Greek Grammars are used".

Free scholars and fee-payers.

"The present Head Master is Mr. John Hamnett, whose salary in consideration of the free boys is £90 per annum together with the interest of Mr. Sewell's legacy and the rent of the house, making in the whole about £113 per annum. This gentleman takes pupils, his terms being thirty-five guineas per annum. The terms for day scholars average about a guinea per quarter. Several of the most respectable merchants in Liverpool have been educated in this School."

The reference to "the present gentleman's predecessor", that is, presumably, Mr. Redhead, is intriguing, but unfortunately we have no information to supplement it. The report of the Charity Commissioners in 1829 tells us much about the school's endowments and finances, but little about its educational activities. It refers to a decision by the acting trustees in 1828

"that in consideration of the increase of salary, the number of boys to be taught in the grammar school should be increased to 50.

By this resolution the freedom of the school has been extended, but the number of 50 was not complete at the time of our inquiry.

The instruction in the school is principally confined to reading, Writing and accounts ; classical instruction, which the master is fully qualified to afford, is not required by the free scholars.

There are some scholars from the town of Prescot who did not apply to be admitted free, and others from the adjoining townships, for whose instruction the master makes his own charge. He has also two boarders, but they are instructed in in his own house.

The school is supplied with copybooks and stationery from the trust funds, and the schoolmaster provides firing, no payment or gratuity being demanded of the free scholars.

The boys are instructed in the church catechism, and are required to attend the Sunday-school of the established church on Sundays. In December they attend the yearly meeting of the persons acting as

29

trustees, and are then examined, and such as appear to deserve it receive a small reward".

The last paragraph above refers, of course, only to the free scholars " of the lower school, with whom the Charity Commissioners were primarily concerned.

Controversy over Schoolwardens.

A controversy arose in 1831 which reveals that the ancient character of the school as a "parish" school had not been forgotten. In a statement of their case compiled by the churchwardens and submitted for counsel's opinion, we are told that the schoolwardens were formerly appointed at the same meeting (on St. Luke's day) at which the select vestry of Eight Men was chosen, "but about 12 or 14 years ago, it being considered that the appointment of the Eight Men as a select Vestry was illegal, they were discontinued, and the persons elected at the same annual meetings to fill the Office of Schoolwardens, being Gentlemen of Fortune in the Neighbourhood of Prescot who paid little or no attention to the duties of the Office, it is supposed the appointment of Schoolwardens was not worth consideration, as since that time no meeting on St. Luke's day has been held, nor any Schoolwardens appointed".

The churchwardens were proposing to revive the St. Luke's day vestry meeting for the purpose of resuming the election of schoolwardens. The trustees of the Prescot charities had, however, made objection on the grounds that the school funds had long ceased to be distinct from those of the charities, and that what rights the schoolwardens may have once possessed had now lapsed. Counsel's opinion, dated 11th October, 1831, was to the effect that the right of electing the schoolwardens " is not lost by fourteen years discontinuance," but that, should the trustees refuse to admit them to participation, "there is no remedy save by resort to the Court of Chancery", and that "many difficulties may occur with respect to the extent of their power and their right of interference with specific funds", which may give rise to "a long litigation, the particular results of which, where so many matters have from lapse of time become obscure, it is impossible to foresee".

Fortunately the problem seems to have been settled by agreement, for in the Churchwardens' Report of 9th April, 1833, it is stated:-

"In concluding their Report, the Churchwardens think it right to notice, that the Wardens elected on St. Luke's day last, for the Free

Grammar School of Prescot, have been admitted by the Trustees to a participation in the government of that establishment, and they trust the arrangement will be beneficial to the School, and satisfactory to all parties interested in its welfare."

A Complaint.

The arrangement, however, does not seem to have proved wholly "satisfactory to all parties", for in 1836 a memorial was addressed to the Commissioners of Education, asking for their intervention on various grounds, namely, that the interference of the officers of the manor in the management of the school was illegal; that the benefits of the school had been arbitrarily restricted to the township of Prescot; that the Vicar had excluded all children of dissenters and Roman Catholics ; that the master was "imbecile" and the assistant put in his place was "an unfit person"; and that 50 boys were too many for one man to teach, especially as he had to take 20 private pupils also in order to eke out the "miserable pittance" given him by the headmaster.†

It is unlikely that the Commissioners of Education would have taken action in this matter, and in all probability the "arrangement" of 1833 was continued. This may have been the scheme in operation in 1854, described in the following extract from *Mannex's Directory of Mid-Lancashire:-*

"The school stands in Fazackerley-street, and is now governed by eight trustees and four school wardens, each of whom nominates six pupils to the lower school at a payment of one shilling per quarter, and one to the higher at half-a-guinea per quarter; and the school endowment amounts to about £150 per annum. The higher school will accommodate 40 and the lower 100 scholars. The Rev. H. D. Baines is the head master and Geoffrey Birtwell the second master."

The Lower School in 1857.

An interesting account of the Lower School under Mr. Birtwell in 1857, written by one of his pupils, the late Mr. William Morton, was published in the *Prescot Weekly Times* , in 1906. There were then ninety scholars, arranged in four classes. The textbooks were the Bible, the Irish National Reader, an Arithmetic, a penny Grammar and the Prayer Book. Both

---

† Footnote :-An abstract of this document is given in the Rev. F. G. Paterson's *History of Prescot* (1908), p. 51, but the original seems to be now lost.

copy-books and slates were used. The books were paid for by the parents in addition to the fee of one shilling per quarter. History and Geography were taught orally, the latter with the aid of wall-maps. The school was commonly known as the "Moss School" from its situation on the old Hackley Moss. Mr. Birtwell, "always pleasant and always effective", inspired an exceptional degree of respect and regard.

Mr. Morton does not refer to the Upper School, save for two small sidelights. First, he mentions that when the Lower School boys were engaged in drill on the ground behind the school "the consequences of a wrong movement on the part of a lad were intensified by the knowledge that 'Baines's boarders' were grinning at him". Secondly, the traditional form of punishment for serious offences, "that had its preliminary in the unbuttoning of the braces", could only be inflicted by the headmaster, "a right, I am sure, our master in the lower school had no wish to deprive him of".

7 - DECLINE AND REVIVAL.

The second half of the nineteenth century, and the opening years of the twentieth, form a period in which the school may be said to have been engaged in a struggle for survival. This was due to a variety of causes : the serious decline of the town's once-famous watch-making industry after 1850; the proximity of Liverpool, where excellent modern schools had by now been established ; the existence, in the same building, of the "Lower School", which in the eyes of the more refined parents appeared rough, and bore the stigma of a "charity school" and, more generally, the development of the idea of state education, which set higher standards than the old endowed schools of this type could as a rule attain unaided.

The loss of the preferences at Brasenose College, to which allusion has been made in our third chapter, must also have materially affected the prospects of the Upper School. This was due to a reorganisation of the finances of the college, ordered by the Oxford University Commissioners in 1862. From this time onward, we hear no more of "boarders" at the school. In this year, the Rev. H. T. Baines, M.A., headmaster since 1851, left to take up a new headship at Hawkshead Grammar School. During the next nine years, the school saw four new headmasters.

The Lowest Ebb.

A report on the school in 1865 by Mr. James Bryce, the representative of the Schools Inquiry Commission, reveals it at probably its lowest ebb. There were about 60 pupils in the Lower School, but in the upper, where there was supposed to be provision for 12 "foundationers" (paying 10/6 quarterly) and 20 other scholars (paying £1/1/6 quarterly), the total had actually shrunk to 12, and of these, only 6 attended on the day of Bryce's visit. "Two, who were in an easy Latin reading book, translated far from well. They tried an arithmetic paper, but made very little of it; their English Grammar and Geography were very weak; and their behaviour and demeanour gave me an unfavourable opinion of the discipline maintained by the head master".

The buildings were, Bryce says, "unsuitable". The Upper and Lower Schools, though virtually independent of each other, were taught in two adjacent rooms, measuring 35 by 12 feet and 35 by 20 feet, respectively. "Both apartments are cheerless and are, or at least look, dirty. There is no master's house ; the present master lives in lodgings, and consequently takes no boarders". There was "a very small playground" by the school.

The governing body still consisted of the trustees of the town charities and the schoolwardens. The headmaster, who "must be a clergyman of the Church of England" - a nineteenth century innovation, this would seem - received a stipend of £130 a year, together with some £36 in fees. There were 42 weeks' schooling in the year, with a week of 27 hours. We are told that "one boy goes to Cambridge in the year", but further details of this exhibition, which may have been of a temporary character only, are not given.

Mr. Bryce recommended, among other things, the re- building of the school, and its complete separation from the Lower School. "A new elementary school should be established, and placed under Government inspection .... and the whole revenue of the foundation might then be devoted to the maintenance of a commercial and classical grammar school" for boys up to the age of 15, but not for those up to 17, as the latter "had better go to Liverpool." Many years were to elapse before these recommendations found fulfilment, unduly modest though they may seem to those familiar with the school of to-day.

Top: The School in High Street.
Below: The Headmaster, John Scholfield, and 'The Upper School', 1890.

Reorganisation of 1876.

For a time, indeed, it seemed to be the Lower School that was destined to survive, at the expense of the Upper. Following the Endowed Schools Act, of 1869, and the Elementary Education Act of 1870, the school was reorganised in 1876 under a new scheme drawn up by the Endowed Schools Commissioners. Mr. D. R. Fearon on behalf of the Commissioners had visited the school in 1874, finding 64 pupils in the Lower School and 29 in the Upper. The Governors of the school, or a majority of them, were desirous of having the Lower School recognised as an Elementary School, and brought under Government inspection, in order to qualify for an annual grant. They were willing for the Upper School to be discontinued, in view of the slight demand, the limited endowments, and the need for more expenditure on Elementary School accommodation.

We may imagine that, as on former occasions, there was much conflict of opinion behind the scenes, with the result that the scheme of 1876, while expressly stating that the school should be carried on "as a Public Elementary School", authorised the maintenance of an "Upper Department, for the purposes of a higher than elementary education". A new body of Governors was constituted, and the endowments were transferred to the Official Trustees of Charitable Funds. Pupils were to pay fees of not more than 9d. a week or, in the Upper Department, not less than £2 or more than £4 a year. The Governors could expend from £20 to £40 in providing scholarships to the Upper Department.

In practice, the scheme of 1876 did not alter the main characteristics of the school. From being (in theory) a Grammar School with a Lower Department, it now became (in theory) an Elementary School with an Upper Department. Actually, it remained very much as before. When Mr. Durnford, an Assistant Commissioner under the Endowed Schools Act, visited the school in 1889, he reported that the scheme of 1876 was not being observed. The Upper School now contained 32 boys, including three free scholars, and the Lower School, conducted as an Elementary School, contained 40. The Upper School was "very successful" but suffered much for want of proper accommodation.

Mr. Scholfield and Canon Mitchell.

Revival had begun. The formation of the Lancashire Watch Company Ltd., in 1889, and of the British Insulated Wire Company Ltd., in 1891, aided it by restoring confidence in the future of the old town. The appointment of Mr. John Scholfield as master of the Upper School in 1882, and of the Rev. Harry Mitchell as Vicar and Chairman of the Governors in 1887, had brought into partnership two men who did much in their respective spheres to restore to the Grammar School its ancient status and to ensure its survival. "Scholfield to me, and I think to most of the boys", writes one of his earliest pupils, Mr. Alexander Appleton, "was the perfect gentleman and perfect schoolmaster - thoroughly capable, patient with the slow, tolerant with the trying, and always just". As for Canon Mitchell, there is still a consensus of opinion on the part of those familiar with the events, commonly expressed in the words "he saved the Grammar School", as truly as, in different circumstances, another vicar, Thomas Mead, had saved the school 300 years earlier.

New Schoolroom, 1890.

From this time on, we witness a reversal of the policy which had actuated the governors prior to 1876. The Grammar School, or Upper School, and not the Lower School, is henceforward regarded as the indispensable element. In 1890 a much-needed extension was provided for the Upper School by the erection of a new schoolroom at the east end of the school, abutting on Moss Street. The cost, £351, was defrayed in part by a loan, in part by voluntary contributions and in part from the proceeds of a bazaar. A photograph of Mr. Scholfield and his 34 scholars in this year is reproduced in these pages.

The prestige of the school must have been considerably enhanced in 1893, when the Countess of Lathom, accompanied by Lady Margaret Cecil, Lady Wilbraham and Lady Carnegie, officiated at the Upper School Prize Distribution.

In 1900 the Governors made the momentous decision to ask for a new scheme to replace that of 1876, and to enable the whole of the endowments to be used for the maintenance, extension and development of the Upper School. Thus, within a quarter of a century, the wheel had turned full circle.

The school was accordingly visited by Mr. A. F. Leach, an Assistant Commissioner under the Endowed School Acts. He found 53 boys in the Upper School, six of them holding scholarships from the Lower, where the number in attendance was 47. The expenditure was in excess of income, and the Governors had been obliged to give a personal guarantee to the Bank.

End of the Lower School.

The new scheme was established by Order dated 7th May, 1901. The school was to be "a secondary school", charging fees of not less than £6 and not more than £12 a year. It was to be "for boys and girls", and boarders might be taken in addition to day scholars "if the Governors think fit". The Governors were to arrange for a yearly examination of the teaching by one or more examiners unconnected with the school.

The same year saw the formal closing of the Lower School, which had for so long been associated with, and had at times even threatened to eclipse, the older foundation. Of the 35 pupils then in attendance, some were admitted to the Upper School, and others transferred to the Elementary School. An interesting relic of the Lower School has been preserved, namely, the Log Book, kept successively by Mr. C. F. Buckham 1877-84, Mr. W. Blaver, 1884-92, and again by Mr. Buckham, 1892-1900. This affords many sidelights on the conditions of schooling in that period.

New Crisis.

In 1902 the Governors considerably improved their financial position by a very judici:.... outlay in the rebuilding of the Church Street property - the original school site - which they let to the Post Office. Their resources were, however, still very inadequate to provide for all the needs of a modern secondary school. At this juncture, a new crisis was precipitated by the Education Act of 1902, which made local authorities - in this case the Lancashire County Council - responsible for secondary education.

The County Council's report of 1904 condemned the school buildings as being "in a far from satisfactory condition" and "quite unsuitable for a modern Secondary Day School". There were 47 scholars, all boys, the scheme of 1901 not having been extended to girls for want of funds. The Governors were anxious to preserve the school, but "it seems extremely doubtful whether such a school is necessary", as girls wanting a secondary education could go to Huyton or St. Helens, and the boys could be transferred to St. Helens. "It is therefore suggested that the Prescot Grammar School be closed, and that if any new School is provided in Prescot, such School should, in the first instance at least, be only a Higher Standard School. If no new School be established, the Endowment . . . . which at present yields about £100 per annum, might be used entirely for the maintenance of Exhibitions tenable at other Secondary schools".

The County's "suggestion" for closing the school was, of course, quite unacceptable to the Governors. The latter, led by Canon Mitchell, rejected the plan in no uncertain terms, and determined to carry on. The County had no power to enforce its recommendations, and so, deferring to the strength of local feeling, it consented to make a grant to the school.

The School in 1906.

His Majesty's Inspectors descended upon the school in 1906 and compiled a detailed report. Though giving the highest praise to Mr. Scholfield, they criticised the general conditions on much the same lines as the County report of 1904. There were 43 scholars, of whom only four were over 14 and only one over 15. All teaching was given in two large classrooms, without partitions or curtains. The headmaster had one assistant. There was no physical training, no playing field, no gymnasium, no library, no laboratories, no manual training.

The school was, however, "pleasantly conducted", the discipline easily maintained without harshness or undue restraint, and the boys earnest and diligent in their work. The Inspectors were in agreement with the County's recommendations of 1904. They did not perceive any necessity for a Secondary School in Prescot. Nevertheless, they concluded, "it may be best to allow the School to continue its present work, as it supplies a local need which could not otherwise be conveniently met". In such case "a good deal of improvement would be needed in the building or preferably the School should be moved to a larger and better site".

Rapid Progress.

This was at once a gesture and a challenge, to which there was an immediate and decisive local response. In the next two years the numbers increased by fifty per cent., and pupils were entered for the Cambridge Junior Local Examination. After the retirement of Mr. Scholfield in 1908, and the appointment of Mr. C. W. H. Richardson, progress continued at a no less rapid pace. The increasing demand for higher education, manifest throughout the country as a whole, was nowhere stronger or more exacting in its demands upon available resources, than at Prescot. Mr. Richardson's task of carrying on the school under the conditions which prevailed until the long deferred rebuilding of 1924, was Herculean, and even Hercules could not have done it better. More astonishing even than the growth in numbers is the record of academic successes achieved in these most difficult circumstances. Between 1908 and 1923, prizes and scholarships to the value of £1,981 and £1,575 were won by Old Boys and by boys from the school, respectively; 34 boys matriculated at the Universities; and 20 Old Boys graduated at the Universities or obtained diplomas, 12 of them with honours or distinction.

The number of scholars had risen to 105 in 1913, and to 238 in 1923.

Rebuilding Scheme of 1913.

The decision to rebuild the school was made in 1913 after the matter had been considered at a local conference under the chairmanship of Sir Henry Hibbert, held in May, 1912, and after His Majesty's Inspectors, at a further inspection in February, 1913, had expressed their approval as follows:-

"The impression formed at the Inspection of 1906 of the position and prospects of the school has been materially modified by the changes which have shown themselves both in the locality and the school since that date. With serious disadvantages of buildings and equipment the Grammar School has doubled its numbers and developed a curriculum of distinctively Secondary School character; and there can be little doubt, if it were transferred to new buildings its chances of success would be greatly enhanced. It is clear that the demand for Secondary education in Prescot and the immediate neighbourhood has substantially increased and the provision of a new Secondary School can no longer be regarded as unnecessary".

The new school decided upon in 1913 was to be for 200 boys and girls, on a site of 51 acres, part of Yew Tree Farm, St. Helens Road, granted by the Earl of Derby on very generous terms. The project had, however, to be laid aside during the war years - 1914-18 - and thereafter, owing to the continued expansion of the school, still more commodious buildings were found to be necessary. The whole of Yew Tree Farm, comprising 26 acres, was acquired, with the object of erecting two schools, for boys and girls respectively, with playing fields adjacent.

In the Wilderness.

Meanwhile the school had overflowed into additional temporary premises in the town, first Harland's shop (now Houghton's) in High Street (1918), next a portion of the Parish Rooms (1919), then the Central Hall in Chapel Street and the Assembly Rooms in High Street (1920). In the school itself, the two schoolrooms (of 1759 and 1890) had each been divided to form two classrooms, whilst the small room (? the Girls' Room of 1786) was used by the staff and by diners, and euphemistically styled the "banqueting hall".

The year 1919 was marked by other notable events, the retirement of Canon Mitchell after a chairmanship of 32 years, the taking over of the school by the Lancashire County Council and its recognition by the Board of Education.

The old endowments were allocated by the County for the maintenance of an additional annual scholarship, the Foundation Scholarship, tenable at the school.

In 1921, the Higher School Certificate was taken for the first time, and a Sixth Form on modern lines thus established. In the same year the Prize Fund was created with the help of generous subscribers, notably Mrs. C. G. Townshend Driffield and Mr. G. Hinde Nisbett.

The Promised Land.

The new school, opened in 1924 by Sir Henry Hibbert, Chairman of the Lancashire County Council, was designed for 290 boys. This was, unfortunately, the period when economy "was the order of the day, and the buildings, though attractive in many respects - and a Promised Land indeed to those who had sojourned in the wilderness of makeshift premises for so long - were consequently only semi-permanent in character. The range was not completed until 1930, when a combined assembly hall and gymnasium, a dining hall and kitchen, and a woodwork room, were provided. Further extensions, including a library, new physics laboratory and geography room, were made in 1939. The projected girls' school, though sorely needed, has not as yet materialised.

Subsequent events and developments will be found recorded with more colour and detail in other parts of this volume. Suffice it to say that at no time has the school been more flourishing than today, despite five years of war. The increase in numbers has steadily continued - the figure is now over 400 - and this has created new problems of accommodation. Whatever is to come in the way of educational reorganisation, the school faces the future with confidence and with resolution to uphold its motto from the words of St. Paul, quoted by its Founder in his will of 1544 - *Futuram Civitatem Inquirimus.*

Charles W.H. Richardson, and Staff. 1937.
Back - Miss D.M. Huckle, J.E. Hawthorne, G. Dixon, H.M. Scott, G. Drewry, F.A. Bailey,
J.J. Robinson, R.B. Sykes.
Front - E.C. Wood, F.S.D. Stevenson, C.W.H. Richardson, H. Chant, J. Hammond.

R. Spencer Briggs and Staff.
Left - Right: G. Dixon, H. Chant, J.E. Hawthorne. F.S.D. Stevenson, Miss D.M. Huckle,
F.A. Bailey, R.S. Briggs, H.M. Scott, E.C. Wood.

Top: St Helens Road building, circa 1930.
Centre: As above, circa 1949. Note air-raid shelters, centre right.
Bottom: Prescot School, Knowsley Park Lane, 1993.

PART 2

The History of
PRESCOT GRAMMAR SCHOOL and PRESCOT SCHOOL

1944 - 1968 A PERIOD OF GROWTH   *Geoffrey Dixon*

Mr Bailey's history written in 1944 finishes on a note of hope. The school was flourishing, the numbers increasing, the academic standards rising. Mr Richardson had undoubtedly saved the school from extinction and Mr Briggs given it order and organisation and brought it into line with other grammar schools. During his reign the school gained an increasing number of Oxbridge entries and a frequent sprinkling of open scholarships. It was his encouragement that persuaded Mr Bailey to compile the history of the school, based upon his original research into local history.

Between the wars Liverpool council estates gradually crept nearer and nearer Prescot. Consequently the population of the school underwent a subtle change. From being country-based, it now had an element of urban-orientated pupils. New sounds began to be heard in the corridors which contrasted strongly with the local accents. The two elements began to tolerate, if not fully to understand each other. The result of this mixture was entirely beneficial.

400th Anniversary

The celebration of the quatercentenary was a happy event, despite the restrictions imposed by wartime conditions. More important, it saw the establishment of a scholarship fund from which generations of former pupils have benefited. From this fund, raised by private subscription, upwards of £400 was awarded annually to boys proceeding to university. Owing to the efforts of the chairman of the governors, Canon O.L. Martin, the school's connection with King's College, Cambridge and Brasenose College, Oxford was re-established and in both places Prescotians can earn special status.

The war brought its restrictions and shortages, its partings and its sadnesses, but Prescot was fortunate that it was nominated neither a reception nor an evacuation area. We still had sole use of our buildings and were not transported en bloc to the depths of the countryside. After the air-raid shelters were built, education was continued as normally as possible under the difficult conditions. Staff joined the armed forces and were replaced by temporary members, many of them ladies. With tolerance an good humour, Prescot survived better than most and emerged from the ordeal stronger than ever and ready to face the post-war world with increased confidence: this despite the distant but ominous rumblings of danger ahead.

The early post-war years saw many changes of staff. Those outside the grammar school service seemed anxious to get in, while those inside seemed anxious to get out. Younger staff, having experienced command in the forces sought promotion in other schools. With the return of stability, the future of the grammar schools in general appeared rosy indeed. Former grammar school pupils were making their mark upon out natural life. Increasingly, they became leaders in politics, the church, the learned professions, business and industry. Was the Establishment becoming anxious ?

Education Act, 1944

The year 1944 also saw the passing of an act which had a profound effect upon the school; its logical consequences are still being felt. It promised 'secondary education for all'. It did this at a stroke by omitting the distinctive terms, 'grammar' , 'modern', and 'technical'. All post-primary schools were now to be called 'secondary' The former terms, however, were for some time used unofficially.

The great public schools were not touched, thus, as one cynic put it, 'making democracy safe for the public schools'. 'Aided', 'controlled' and 'direct grant' schools retained their status, but Prescot, in company with hundreds of others, was not so designated. A few with rich endowments became independent. In such schools as Prescot tuition fees were abolished, and entry was solely by examination. Known popularly as the '11+' examination, it was viewed with increasing disfavour, despite the entrance tests at 12+ and 13+. In consequence, also, the preparatory department was phased out. Although for many years the school superficially appeared little changed, the full implications of the act were increasingly obvious.

Endowments

When Lancashire County Council took over the school, it also took over the endowments, which at that time were worth very little. In lieu, they established an internal foundation scholarship open to fee-payers. Fees having been abolished, in 1958 the school properties were returned to the school, and a separate board of Foundation Governors was empowered to control these funds and to disburse the income under a special trust deed. The value of the endowments, considerably increased, now generated an income exceeding £2,500 per annum. This was an asset the school soon learned to appreciate and use. It enabled the school to seek a property suitable for use as an outdoor pursuits centre. Of this, more later.

41

Rebuilding

In 1955 The Prescot Girls' Grammar School was opened. It was housed in buildings which certainly put the boys' wooden building to shame. However, in the early sixties it was decided to rebuild the boys' school and a start was made on a splendid new hall and specialist rooms. In 1963 Mr Briggs retired and within a year he died. He never saw the new buildings which were to be the first phase of a four-stream grammar school. In his honour the new hall was named after him. The second phase of the new school was already planned and looked most attractive. Was the new school about to enter a second 'promised land' ?

Reorganisation

It was at this time that the shadow of reorganisation fell across the school, and Mr J.M. Brown, recently appointed head of a grammar school, was called upon to attend a series of meetings of the working party, which eventually recommended that the school become a six/seven form entry comprehensive school, one of three in the area. At this time streaming was replaced by setting in individual subjects, but this was of no avail in stemming the tide which was flowing strongly in favour of comprehensive education. The grammar schools were said to be elitist. Their education was thought to be too formal and academic, a criticism which seems ironic, in view of the noises emerging from the Establishment twenty years later.

If the grammar schools had been asked to defend themselves they would surely have claimed that they provided the children of parents of modest means the opportunity to compete with the more privileged. Perhaps in this they had been too successful for their own good. Perhaps they were too conscious of their own virtue to defend themselves with sufficient vigour but the politicians were determined to sweep them away in favour of comprehensive schools. The attitude of many people was ambivalent . With sublime lack of logic, they did not wish to lose their grammar schools but were determined to reject selection, the system which had made those schools so successful.

It is a profitable exercise today to recall what went on in those schools before they were abolished. What was the grammar school ethos ? Certainly, it embraced a respect for learning and scholarship for their own sake. It stressed the value of discipline and hard work ....but it also encouraged the use of the creative imagination. These schools were not inward-looking and studied the modern world in addition to the past. They were still developing when they came to such an abrupt end. Contrary to the propaganda spread by our opponents (and we had many, some hoping to profit by our demise), lessons did not consist of the learning of lists of facts, history of dates, mathematics and science of formulae, English of grammatical rules, foreign languages of irregular verbs. Subjects were taught in the whole and in depth. Nor was the syllabus compartmentalised. We had a whole range of societies, all meeting out of school time. Our concerts, our plays, became significant events in our local communities. We do not claim perfection but we had our standards. Overseas visitors, many from the United States of America, were amazed at the range and depth of our activities. The grammar school sixth forms, along with our junior schools, were the star achievements of our educational system.

On a purely personal note, I regard myself as being particularly fortunate in spending my forty-two years at Prescot Grammar School during its hey-day. I leave it to others to chart the passage of the school through the troubled waters ahead.

1971 - A MOMENT IN TIME   *John C. S. Weeks*

Qualities of endurance and determination mark the years that are recorded in this volume. For those who are involved in the day-to-day teaching and administrative programme of the present school it is easy to feel the confidence and vitality that are ingrained as a consequence of history. Continuity of ideals seep through to staff and pupils and Mr Bailey's essay consolidates and verifies what we absorb.

At the moment the school is strong and secure. The strength comes from its traditions; the security from the protection offered by the state system. We have no worries, as our predecessors had, that we shall fail to exist as a school; we only wonder what our exact function is to be.

State provision is secure, but it is also parsimonious. Our financial heritage, in which we are so fortunate, offers us great opportunities. Not only are Old Prescotians helped at university, and the major school societies supported when necessary, but also Sixth-formers benefit from travel scholarships which take them to all corners of Europe on research topics of their choice. Particularly has the whole school profited by the acquisition of White Hart House at Dent, high in the Yorkshire Dales. This, a community and field study centre, already has its own core of activities and by its very existence encourages a wider perception among us.

Our Sixth-form has expanded like all others and our curriculum with it. The emphases of our special interests, in and out of the classroom, change with the initiative and stimulus offered by the staff, but our aim is as it always has been, to achieve educational integrity in all fields. We have a right to be proud of the variety and excellence of our achievements.

In the previous pages we read of the many pressures that have laid heavily on the school in the past - the paucity of buildings, the shortage of money, the brooding anxiety of war. Now we are subject to the vicissitudes of educational and social fashion as never before, which affect every school in the country, but which are no less demanding because of that. Technology and new techniques help us spread our wings, while government stringency clips them. Our senior pupils are now adults by law, and increasingly the educational generation gap is visible at sixteen rather than eighteen, as the school-leaving age is raised to coincide with the school-leaving certificate. The problems this creates are not easy to solve in our existing buildings.

The reorganisation planned in 1965 may still be effected, but it is not necessaily the most valid solution for the area, and so we wait a little nervously as the authorities do their sums yet again. Whatever the result of their deliberations there will be a need for rapid adaptation, for we will become either a neighbourhood comprehensive serving Prescot and Whiston, or we will cater for a more restricted age-group from a wider area. Whichever of these is the solution the new school is bound to retain a great deal of value from the past, and Prescot should continue to have pride in its ancient educational foundation.

1971 - 1977 CHANGE AND AMALGAMATION   *John C. S. Weeks*

Pragmatic Change

The movement towards comprehensive education in Lancashire was well launched by the early 1970s but, with hindsight, it is now obvious that any proposals for change at Prescot were being held until the very last. Two problems faced the County Council. One was the need for a totally new school complex to replace the wooden hutted buildings in St Helens Road; the other, which ruled the first, was uncertainty about the catchment for any comprehensive school in the Prescot area and the viability of the neighbouring schools. This was the cause of some tinkering with ideas about Sixth Form Colleges, Senior and Junior High and every sort of combination. In the end, it was not educational principle that guided the political decisions but pure pragmatism. Rainford High School became a comprehensive school in 1971 thus depriving PGS of the valued Eccleston end of its widespread catchment. The resulting tilt away from the St Helens suburbs towards the environs of Liverpool was portrayed by the switch of emphasis among the accents in the classrooms.

Local Government Reorganisation

This predated the dramatic change of local government reorganisation in 1974, following the Maude Report. There can have been few schools in the north-west so affected as Prescot. Fifty years after the opening of the new school buildings, Prescot was summarily removed from Lancashire. The formation of the new Boroughs of Knowsley and St Helens placed a local government boundary right through the middle of the games fields. With one sweep of the bureaucrat's pen the school was severed from its eastern catchment. The old Whiston Secondary Modern school came within the St Helens boundary and PGS in Knowsley. Whiston became Rainhill High School absorbing all the children from that prosperous and supportive corner. Whatever the arguments for and against grammar schools, there was no possibility of the survival of Prescot as a grammar school when over 50% of the feeder primary schools containing a higher proportion of 11+ passes had been transferred to a different Local Education Authority. Suddenly, the boys' and girls' grammar schools together were on an island. Their catchment was reduced to the old town of Prescot, parts of Whiston and the burgeoning estates of Huyton and Knowsley. The only solution deemed possible (rather than the Sixth Form College which would have suited our academic traditions much more appropriately) was for the two grammar schools to combine and become a comprehensive school.

Amalgamation

Two major changes were required of both schools. They had to become both co-educational and comprehensive at the same time. In its initial stages at least, paradoxically, the marriage was helped by its being a two-site school. We learned to live together: slowly but happily. Gradually the ethos which had been the strength of both schools filtered through the new comprehensive school. Tribute is due to the composure with which the staff accepted change and their enthusiasm for the wider curriculum which they provided for the fully comprehensive intake of pupils. Throughout this difficult period the school continued to maintain its hold on a considerable reputation. Its willingness to embrace the advantages of the new CSE examination for some of its pupils, which fitted neatly with its belief in setting rather than streaming established so many years before, meant that it was better prepared for change than many other grammar schools at the time. The staff had an open-mindedness not often the case in such institutions. At this time it was decided to commemorate the school's founder by naming the St Helens Road site after Gilbert Lathum. It was tragic that so shortly afterwards the old wooden buildings were to be destroyed by fire, never to be replaced.

Continuing Excellence

White Hart House continued to flourish as the school's field study centre until it was sold in 1988. Hundreds of pupils benefited from its facilities and its success left a deep and abiding mark on a school which always searched beyond its own walls for the education of the whole child.

The Foundation Governors' generosity was not restricted to this one investment. Many senior boys, and later girls, were to benefit from the University Scholarships and Travel Scholarships. These were the stimulants of and rewards for much intellectual endeavour and initiative among the pupils particularly those gaining entry to our co-foundation, Brasenose College, Oxford and to two Cambridge colleges, St Catharine's and King's.

I hold deep personal and professional memories of colleagues who so helped maintain the strong comitment in the future of the school. Retaining close contact with my successor, Peter Barlow, I see and know the school to be in excellent heart.

1977 - 1994 PRESCOT SCHOOL   *Peter A. Barlow*

The National Scene

It was in 1976 that James Callaghan, the Prime Minister, in a speech at Ruskin College called for a 'Great Debate' on the current state of education in the country and how it should be changed to meet the challenges of the years ahead. A number of themes emerged to dominate thinking in education and training right into the 1990s. What is an appropriate curriculum for children of all abilities? Who should have influence and control in the schools of the country? How should education be resourced and how could value for the money invested be ensured? To what extent should market forces enter education? How should schools be made accountable and to whom?

The Education Act of 1986, dealing with School Government and

Organisation was followed by the even weightier Act of 1988 which initiated fundamental reforms including Open Enrolment of pupils, Local Management of Schools whereby governing bodies were increasingly responsible for their own budgets and staffing, Grant Maintained Schools and most important of all a National Curriclum for all from the age of 5 to 16. In 1993 came the last of this mighty trio of Education Acts to consolidate much of what had appeared earlier. It encouraged choice and diversity in schools, enhanced parental choice and in particular it determined the relationship between schools and Local Authorities. Much of this was imposed by the Government and the mid-1980s suffered a damaging withdrawal of goodwill by the teachers' unions which saw the need for change but often disagreed with its pace and direction. The governors, parents and teachers at Prescot welcomed a number of the changes but innovation overload was severe. It would have been misleading to continue to use the wrod 'debate'. Management in the school, while sustaining a high rate of change, had to be very sensitive to just how much the staff in the school could stand.

The full inspection of the school by Her Majesty's Inspectors in June 1992 gave an independent and thoroughly professional assessment of how the school was responding to all the changes. Their Report found the school with many strengths, of committed staff working in difficult circumstances, of good management and of strong links with local industry. It also mentioned the need to improve the level of pupils' achievement and to encourage more varied teaching techniques in some subjects. The Report highlighted two great concerns which have permeated earlier pages in this history, the inadequacy of resources and the poor accommodation. However, the Inspection found the school generally in good heart and not complacent about the need for further improvements.

The Local Scene

In its long history the school has on a number of occasions faced a very uncertain future but the academic year of 1977-1978 tested the resilience of the pupils, staff and parents to a remarkable degree. The greater part of the 1924 building at Lathum Wing, the former boys' grammar school, was destroyed in two major fires in February and July 1978. The Spencer Briggs building opened in 1965 was found to have serious structural faults and the Knowsley Chief Education Officer proposed that the school should be phased out as soon as possible to assist the Borough's problem of falling rolls. This was indeed a baptism of fire for the new Headmaster.

As separate schools, Prescot Grammar School and Prescot Girls' Grammar School had been virtually isolated from the problem of falling rolls. When

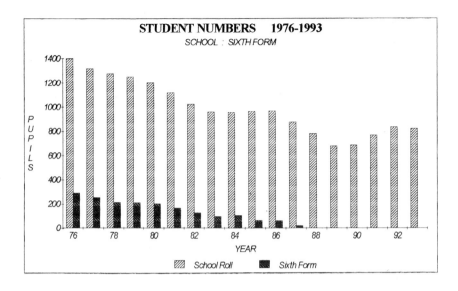

STUDENT NUMBERS 1976-1993
SCHOOL : SIXTH FORM

Legend: School Roll, Sixth Form

Based on January figures

1976   Amalgamation of Prescot Grammar School
        and Prescot Girls' Grammar School

1982   School becomes Comprehensive

1984   Knowsley Tertiary College open

1986   Last year for entry into Lower Sixth Form

For a full explanation of this chart see
The Local Scene (page 47)

amalgamated as a single 11 - 18 comprehensive school with a designated reduced intake and only three official feeder primary schools, all in Prescot, the bracing and at times chilling winds of competition were inevitable.

While 210 new pupils were accepted each year, by September 1979 the Sixth Form, 217 strong, came entirely from within the school. Four years later the total population of the school had settles at about 950 and this roll may well have been maintained but a significant decline commenced in September 1986 as the Sixth Form was phased out and a Tertiary College developed in Knowsley.

The school would not have survived had it relied solely upon about 80 pupils (but falling each year) from the Prescot primary schools. Pupils were entering in Year One from more than twenty primary schools. By the end of the decade up to 70% of the intake came from schools beyond Prescot. Only 4% travelled from beyond Knowsley.

The response of the Authority to the most severe falling rolls of any Local Authority in Britain was to propose closures, amalgamations and reorganisations. The consequences of the first fire at Lathum Wing in February 1978 were perceived by the Chief Education Officer as an opportunity to recommend closure of the school. The idea gained little support but it was followed immediately by a proposal to amalgamate the school with Higher Side Comprehensive School in Whiston. Rumour had it that should this scheme fail one or other of the schools would close. A Parents' Action Group was formed to fight for the school's survival. In January 1982 the proposal to amalgamate the schools was thrown out by the Department of Education and Science. Later in the same year instead of again recommending closure, a most radical reorganisation of schools was advanced with several 11 - 16 comprehensives feeding a single Tertiary College. The staff, governors and parents of Prescot School were very divided on the issue but following all the uncertainty of the previous five years the majority, while not loking the proposals, considered them a more acceptable arrangement for the good of all the pupils of Knowsley than the schemes so far discussed. It was in 1921 that Prescot Grammar School established a Sixth Form; in its modern sense, Prescot School would lose this inheritance.

In 1977 there were twenty-four 11 - 18 comprehensive schools in Knowsley; by 1990 there were eleven, mainly 11 - 16 schools and one tertiary college, Knowsley Community College. Prescot School was one of the survivors and in September 1990 there was a rapid rise in the student roll partly owing to the closure of a school in Stockbridge Village. This rise was sustained during the next year but levelled off in September 1992. Evidence was appearing that the split site and poor buildings were discouraging some parents from choosing Prescot for their children.

However, in 1993 the Local Authority at last made a determined effort to concentrate the school on one site with adequate buildings. This was to be achieved by the sale of the St Helens Road site and the provision of alternative playing fields off Knowsley Park Lane. To what extent this was the result of parents of the pupils of the school opting to remain in the Authority in a ballot for Grant Maintained Status held in December 1992 is a matter of argument. Nevertheless, at last the often repeated wish of the Governors was being acted upon. With this good news and a greater commitment to marketing, the school could anticipate rising rolls once more.

The Curriculum.

The need to provide a curriculum appropriate to all pupils coming from a very broad academic range and one which equipped each for life at the end of the twentieth and early twenty-first centuries was central to the activities of the school. In September 1977, virtually all classes were coeducational with the first three years at Lathum and the remainder at Park Wing. The school had to retain that which was good from the past and the staffs of both the boys' and girls' grammar schools had much to give They also, for the most part, responded to the wider challenge of a comprehensive school. In 1978, five pupils went up to Oxford or Cambridge Universities while some eleven-year-old pupils were entering the first year with a reading age of seven.

The rush to mixed ability teaching was questioned and revised. Broader options leading to a full range of GCE and CSE examinations were agreed, the 'Open Sixth' being established in the late 1970s. Throughout the decade the local environment and community were seen as an enriching resource and this became a crucial element in the comprehensive curriculum.

A particular emphasis was put on links with the business community. As far as BICC was concerned this involved the formation of a liaison committee which did much to bring the school departments and the company together. The school and BICC mounted a 'Technology Today' exhibition in 1978, which included the new fibre optics, and the Economists in the Sixth Form organised seminars for the company's middle managers including union representatives. Particularly significant was the development of Vocational Courses at first in the Sixth Form and then in 1983 in the Fourth and Fifth years. A Foundation Course in 'Information Technology' was piloted by the school and was eventually taken over by the City an Guilds of London Institute (CGLI). All these courses attracted considerable attention including a visit to the school in December 1983 by the Secretary of State for Education, Sir Keith Joseph. In 1984 the school was among the first fifty secondary schools in the country to receive the prestigious Schools Curriculum Award for its links with the community. The Technical and Vocational Education Initiative (TVEI) was launched by the Government in 1983 and for several years Knowsley remained aloof but when the school was allowed to take advantage of the funding the staff was in a good position, the school having pioneered vocational courses, to adapt the school's curriculum to the new TVEI emphases. Furthermore, the school staff played a very active part in the Authority's National Curriculum study groups. For example, they were largely responsible for the production of the guidelines booklet on 'The Roman Empire' and gave a lead to others on Equal Opportunities.

The CGLI phased out its Foundation courses because they were geared to the less academically gifted students and as the GCSE and then the National Curriculum developed it became difficult to run strictly vocational courses for 15 and 16 year-olds. The school's response was to encourage all departments to foster links with the business community, to stress work experience for pupils and staff and to take every opportunity to weave a vocational thread into each course.

Throughout the 1980s the school was largely successful in retaining the courses it valued and in responding to the new examination requirements. As far as the curriculum was concerned, Knowsley did its best to build a partnership with the headteachers in its schools, most significantly in 1983, by developing a curriculum-led staffing policy. Without this, a strict application of the pupil/teacher ratio (PTR) of about 16 : 1 in the late 1970s would have frustrated innovation, damaged the education of children in one of the most economically and socially deprived local authorities in the country and caused an even harsher schools' rationalisation programme. By 1988 the PTR at 13.9 : 1 was indeed generous although finance for anything other than staffing was strictly limited.

The 1988 Education Reform Act initiated, for the first time in this country, a National Curriculum which introduced the most radical changes in education, perhaps since the Education Act of 1944. It also brought in Local Management of Schools (LMS) which in Knowsley seriously disadvantaged any school with significantly rising rolls. This hit Prescot School hardest of all. Every effort was made to protect the curriculum and develop courses within the framework of the new curriculum - but at what cost to the staff ! When the school was formally inspected in June 1992, the first such inspection since the 1930s, the PTR had risen to an unacceptable 17.89 : 1. Once again the resilience of all was put to the test. Too often the Governors wrestled with financial rather than curricular problems and too often the National Curriculum in the school was circumscribed by financial considerations. The Inspectors found the unlikely combination of an efficient school with a deficit budget. Knowsley Authority was able to give little more than words of sympathy and some help in facilitating the early retirement of members of staff.

Despite all difficulties visitors, student teachers and new teachers all spoke of good morale in the staff-room. Although driven by the National Curriculum to concentrate on their individual subjects, teachers did their best to ensure that cross-curricular themes including Economic and Industrial Understanding as well as Information Technology received due attention. In 1992 the school received and Education Industry Partnership Award for a major cross-curricular project.

The Wider Curriculum

To place so much emphasis on curricular matters might be interpreted as ignoring the pastoral well-being of the pupils but the best foundation for personal development is in a good curriculum suited to the needs of each individual. Both the boys' and the girls' schools benefited from rich and varied programmes of extra-curricular activities. While there were changes to accommodate the needs of pupils, Prescot School was able to maintain much of this commitment although the pressure on the time of teachers over the last few years caused some retrenchment.

Music and sport remained very strong; the sports teams regularly winning the Knowsley trophies. This strength should be set against a national scene in which team sports among teenagers did not enjoy their former support and the totally inadequate sports facilities which could easily have discouraged a less committed specialist staff. Some pupils gained county and even national recognition. Soon after the amalgamation of the two schools, the orchestra became so large that audiences in the Park Wing were necessarily restricted. Programmes of Music and Dance were most successful . Drama, though flourishing in the classroom, was not able to provide large productions beyond the mid-1980s. As a result of this arrangement it appeared that several pupils were encouraged to appear in a number of television programmes including 'soap operas'.

Outdoor pursuits could have been discouraged by the sale of the field study centre at Dent in 1988. It had been the intention of the Foundation Governors to purchase a larger property in a more remote part of the country. However, the refusal of the Planning Authority to grant change-of-use to a prospective property in Bala was an unwelcome surprise. An alternative property was rented and the £44,000 achieved by the sale of Dent was wisely invested while the search for appropriate accommodation continued. Eventually, Tai'n-y-graig, a farm near Pentre-llyn-Cymer in Snowdonia was purchased in 1992 at a cost of £75,000. In the meantime, Outdoor Pursuits had continued with particularly important residential weeks for older pupils. It is intended to resume the programmed visits which had been so successful as soon as the property in Wales is renovated.

Foreign visits continue to enjoy wide support. French and German having equal status in the school, visits to Vouziers in France and Moers in Germany have done much to encourage the study of both subjects and the European Dimension. Ski trips and a Portuguese exchange have been very successful.

Finally, there are those extensions to the curriculum which allow pupils to study their own particular interests in greater depth. This is made possible by the willingness of the teachers to devote their lunch-times to the work. Art, Business Studies, Information Technology, Latin and certain Science courses have been offered for a number of years. Committed pupils are thus enabled to make the most of their talents.

Looking Back to Our Future.

"Memories, sir." So said a Sixth Former as I approached a group surveying the smouldering ashes of the buildings of Lathum Wing. It was 1978, fifty-four years after the 'semi-permanent' buildings had been established in St Helens Road; at last the Prescot Grammar School was accommodated on one site. History was now repeating itself and again there had commenced a period of split sites, of promises, of inadequate capital and maintenace grants - and frustrations. It was fortunate that many of the school archives had been duplicated and the copies securely stored in Huyton Library. While the parchment recording the Grant of Arms to the school was retrieved from a safe amid the smoking ruins, the war memorials were no more. Fire had destroyed the buildings: it could not deprive the school of its endowments.

In 1989 the Charity Commissioners approved a new scheme entitled The Prescot School Endowment Fund'. It retained all the benfits of the earlier Grammar School Fund but gave the Foundation Governors a little more flexibility in the application of the funds. Approximately £12,000 annually is available to the Governors and at present their order of priorities is :

1.   The managing, maintenance and support of the property of the

Charity.

2.   Travel Scholarships.

3.   Field work and related activities.

4.   Assistance to School departments.

5.   Awards to former pupils under 25 years of age who are resident within 'The Urban District of Prescot'.

As parents find themselves less able to provide financial help, without the support of the Endowment Fund many of the particular benefits enjoyed in the past by individual pupils and the school in general would have withered away. The school would have been unable to support those imaginative and innovative projects which raise the school above he ordinary.

The Four Hundredth Anniversary Scholarship Fund enjoys an annual income of some £2,500 the major portion of which is awarded to former pupils at universities. The fund is limited and a high standard must be maintained by all who gain scholarships, bursaries or grants. Once again, the strong connection between the school and BICC is maintained; not only did the company originally provide a substantial portion of this particular investment, it now manages the Fund and provides two of the Trustees.

As we look back we see other traditions maintained and developing within the school. The Founder's Day celebration in October has been joined by the annual Carol Service in December. In 1992, an updated version of the Prescot Grammar School armorial bearings was adopted and brought into use by the Governors. The Prescot Grammar School Annual Dinner has been joined by a reunion of Prescot Girls' Grammar School. The Prescot School Association of parents continues to give valuable support often under difficult circumstances. The Prescot School Board of Governors which has steered the school through the centuries is now stronger, more active and well led. It is well equipped to take the school forward.

1994 - The 450th ANNIVERSARY of the FOUNDATION

Despite the serious financial difficulties mentioned earlier, the school looks forward over the few remaining months to 1994 with confidence. Challenged it has been in the past and challenged it will be in the future. However, it has proved that the staff, pupils and governors can not only respond creatively but often give a lead for other schools to follow. It is most encouraging that there is

53

every likelihood that the first phase of a new building will be complete in 1994 - financed by the sale of the Lathum Wing site.

1544 - Church Street, 1759 - High Street, 1924 - St Helens Road; it would be singularly appropriate if we are able to say, 1994 - Knowsley Park Lane.

Futuram Civitatem Inquirimus

HEADMASTERS of the SCHOOL from 1882

John Scholfield. *Univ. Lond.*   C.W.H. **Richardson**, M.A.*(Cantab.)*, B.Sc.*(Lond.)*
R.S. **Briggs**, M.A. *(Cantab.)*   M.J.M. **Brown**, M.A. *(Cantab.)*, M.A. *(Oxon.)*
J.C.S. **Weeks**, M.A. *(Cantab.)*   P.A. **Barlow**, B.A.*(Leeds)*, B.Mus.*(Leeds)*

Appendix

THE VERY EARLY DAYS

A John WILLMOTT and W.J. SHEILS

The date of the foundation of Prescot Grammar School was given by F.A. Bailey as 1544, this being the date of the drawing up of the will of Gilbert Lathum. It seems likely that Lathum died in 1546 though it was not until 1552 that his will was proved. The details of that will are set out in Bailey's description of the setting up of the school given elsewhere in this book.

It seems certain that the foundation of Prescot Grammar School cannot be dated much earlier than this. Jordan [1] indicates that in Lancashire, *"There were only three grammar schools founded in the Middle Ages which survived in 1480. The oldest of these was that at Lancaster, subsequently known as the Royal Grammar School.......................................A school was also established at Preston, possibly in 1358, in connection with a chantry....................................The third of the medieval foundations was a grammar school at Middleton, founded in 1412."* On the other hand, there is evidence of the foundation of a grammar school in 1507 in the parish of Prescot at Farnworth. This school was established by the great Tudor churchman, William Smyth, Bishop of Lincoln. Jordan gives details of the foundation of this school.

However, Jordan is less certain about the date of the establishment of Prescot Grammar School. He suggests that the school at Prescot might have been established as early as the beginning of the sixteenth century. Jordan indicates that the school had been a struggling institution *"supported by outright gifts, fines and fees"* for several decades. He interprets Lathum's will to mean that Gilbert Lathum *"undertook to fashion the institution into a free and endowed grammar school"* the implication being that the school already existed in 1544. It is possible that the school at Prescot had been a chantry school for Jordan asserts that *"the too-much maligned Chantry Commissioners in Lancashire, as elsewhere, preserved every educational endowment and whenever possibly greatly strengthened the existing schools by ordering the whole of the mixed chantry to be diverted to the latter purpose."*

Jordan's account of the revitalising of existing institutions in this way is also representative of what was happening elsewhere in England and in Lancashire in particular. His view is supported by Haigh [2] who pointed out that at the beginning of the sixteenth century there were several schools linked to chantry foundations in Lancashire and at several of them *"the chantry priest was also the school master."* However, Haigh indicates the possible earlier existence of the school at Prescot for he mentions that in *"1543, Humphrey Ogle, a Prescot man, founded two Brasenose scholarships with preference for candidates first from Prescot and then from the*

Diocese of Chester." Presumable Ogle had it in mind that such scholarships would be awarded to suitable candidates at a school already in existence in Prescot.

For the period of 1544 and beyond, Jordan's account of the development of Prescot Grammar School accords with that described by Bailey as does that of Haigh. Indeed, the latter draws upon the published work of Bailey.

[1] W.K. Jordan *The Social Institutions of Lancashire,* Chetham Society, (1962)

[2] C. Haigh, *Reformation and Resistance in Tudor Lancashire,* Cambridge University Press, (1975)

PRESCOT GIRLS' GRAMMAR SCHOOL
A Privileged Community

F. Barbara SMITH

Before 1955, the pupils of Lancashire Division 14 and of the Huyton-with-Roby Excepted District who won places at grammar schools had to travel to such schools as Cowley in St Helens, Wade Deacon in Widnes or to those in Liverpool. Secondary modern school provision in the area was adequate and the boys had the opportunity of grammar school education in Prescot, but the girls were not provided for locally.

In October, 1955, Prescot Girls' Grammar School was at last opened on what later became known as the Park Site. Its wide and varied catchment area remained until local government reorganisation in 1974. Planned as three-form-entry and later becoming four-form-entry, the first intake into the new school was a of eighty-eight eleven-year-olds streamed on entrance. There were five assistant teachers. The school thus had the undoubted advantage of growing from embryo and had no difficulty in establishing an ethos of its own.

The site was well favoured. Adjacent to Lord Derby's estate and before the construction of the by-pass, it was quiet and rural. The pleasant grounds and sports fields were attended by a full-time groundsman. The building, at first com-prising just classrooms, library, gymnasium and administrative offices, was light and airy. However, in the early years the peace was often shattered by building work as the first stage was completed with the addition of the assembly hall, practical rooms, some laboratories and, later ....a staff-room. By 1961 the much-needed new east wing was added. This provided further laboratory and practical accommodation. Three demountable classroom units had already been placed on the north side to alleviate over-crowding.

The first headmistress, Miss Joan Keay, had clear ideas about the kind of education to be offered and the school rapidly achieved high academic standards. The girls became part of a happy, orderly and hard-working community and their results at Ordinary Level in the General Certificate of Education were markedly above the national average in the great majority of subjects. At Advanced Level too, as the years passed, excellent results were obtained: many girls went on to universities and colleges and into the professions.

When I succeeded Miss Keay to the headship in 1968 there were 685 pupils on roll, 120 in the sixth form and a staff of thirty-seven. At this stage there was little or no contact between the girls' and the boys' schools although the governors of the girls' school had been pressing for their school to benefit jointly from the Foundation funds. This was eventually agreed by the Charities Commission. Gradually the two schools began to enjoy joint activities.

The pupils were offered a liberal education and every opportunity for personal development. Set as it was in an established community, the school was appreciated by the better-off and poorer parents alike and received much support.

Growth continued: in 1970 and afterwards, the roll increased to 750 and the staff to forty-two. The curriculum and organisation were under constant review; CSE courses began to be offered. To the already impressively wide choice of activities and visits arranged by an enthusiastic staff was added the important element of community service with the elderly and with deprived children.

Another area of expansion was music. In 1973, 100 pupils were receiving instrumental training and 15 individual voice tuition; the orchestra, choirs and folk-groups flourished. In addition to concerts, productions such as *My Fair Lady* were presented. Thus, when the two schools were merged, both had much to offer and an outstanding music department was created.

The girls' grammar school provided fine opportunities for success in mathematics and the sciences as well as in subjects then often thought to be more easily mastered by girls. Not surprisingly, governors and others hoped that the comprehensive system might also be on a single sex basis. This was not to be and increasingly time was spent on planning the merger of the two schools in 1975 - a change which, in the event, brought many mutual benefits. A decision to allow staff to retain joint positions of seniority freed their minds from anxiety about their personal situation. The time available was well occupied with curriculum planning for all levels of ability, especially with the creation of courses suitable for very weak pupils.

For a period of twenty years and more, the twenty per cent girls who won places at Prescot Girls' Grammar School had certainly become members of a privileged community.

THE FIRES OF 1978
P A BARLOW 10:03:93

"It was like an inferno - there was nothing the firemen could do except save the other buildings". These were the words of a neighbour to a reporter from the local newspaper.

The fire had started in the south-east corner of the school at approximately 4 a.m. on Wednesday, 1st February, 1978. Speading rapidly through the timber structure it consumed class-rooms at the rear of the school, along the east wing and to the room originally the Art room; eight rooms in addition to the Library. Six hundred and thirty pupils arrived only to see steam rising from the charcoaled remains of much of their school. Plastic covers to the lamp-post lights had melted into weird shapes; broken glass was everywhere and the remaining rooms were coated in a sticky black deposit.

There were three days before the half-term holiday. All the pupils from the affected wing were sent home and there began the formidable task of clearing up, restoring services and providing alternative accommodation within ten days. The various Knowsley Services and BICC Ltd. were extremely helpful although there was a powerful move by the Chief Education Officer to plan for a school in Prescot of 4 or 5 forms of entry plus seventy-five Sixth Formers. The school's management team made the first priority the acquisition of replacement, albeit mobile, buildings. The headmaster spent many hours endeavouring to convince politicians that only a 7-form entry comprehensive school would be viable unless additional resources were allocated. The Policy and Resources Sub-Committee eventually supported this proposal although the sudden enthusiasm in favour of building such a school on the Park Site soon began to wane.

The pupils returned after the half-term break. A number of 'mobiles' were in place and the teaching rooms in the Spencer Briggs building which had been closed owing to structural faults were 'AKRO'-propped. Huge wooden railway sleepers criss-crossed each room and supported metal props at six-foot intervals to provide a most extraordinary teaching environment. This was not to be the end of our difficulties.

In the early hours of Tuesday, 11th July, in the same year neighbours were awakenedby the sound of breaking glass and the crackling of burning timbers. Within a period described as a few minutes, hot ashes were landing in the gardens of the houses in St Helens Road. This time the front of the school was ablaze. All the rooms in this portion including the gymnasium (formerly the Assembly Hall) and some of the accommodation along the west corridor were reduced to their foundations with a tangled mass of girders and pipes topping the devastation. Radiators and the old school safe stood among blackened heaps of books, equipment and pupil records. The school had lost its administration rooms, its staff-room, its gymnasium and changing facilities, two more class-rooms and some of the toilets. Disbelief reigned among staff and pupils. Others were 'not surprised.'

Pupils in Years 1 and 2 were despatched to Park Wing because not all those in the Fifth and Upper Sixth Forms were still at school. Somehow, Year 3 managed to remain at Lathum in the face of great adversity until the end of term.

After the two fires in 1978.

i.   The hall/gym. from the stage looking across the quad.

ii.   Main entrance.

iii.   Hall on right: view towards main entrance. Chimneys of fireplaces in Head's study & staff rooms.

Everyone, including the governors, busied themselves through the month of August. It was a particular tribute to both staff and pupils that they commenced the Autumn term in September undaunted on a site which visitors often found depressing, Proposals to disperse pupils to other schools had been resisted, the Spencer Briggs Hall had become a gymnasium and there was a medley of mobile class-rooms served by an elevated walk-way above the heating pipes. Few would have imagined that not until 1988 would most of this temporary accommodation be transferred to Park Wing and, if present plans are fulfilled, that the anniversary year of 1994 will see the last pupil leave the Lathum Wing in St Helens Road.

RECOLLECTIONS OF THE PAST

> There follow ten short passages by former pupils. Those by Scholfield, Best, Maynard, Wainwright and Smith are abridged from the first edition. The remainder were commissioned in 1993 for inclusion in the present edition. None the worse for a few light-hearted moments, they recall various aspects of the life-style of the school from the end of the nineteenth century to the recent past.

1 - **W.F. Scholfield,** M.A., O.B.E., (1893-97.)

> *"The Child is father of the man*
> *And I could wish my days to be*
> *Bound each to each by natural piety."*

From the fact that this quotation from Wordsworth's ode introduces my remarks on my school-days at Prescot Grammar School during my father's headmastership, it would be a mistake to infer that English Literature in general or the study of Wordsworth in particular formed a particular feature of the curriculum at that time. This quotation expresses in as short a form as possible, I think, the idea underlying the general atmosphere of teaching in those days.

I arrived at the school very shortly after the new school-room had been built, and I can recollect my first impressions of the great newness and orderliness of everything and the convenience of the desks. These extended in three parallel rows the whole length of the well-lit school-room and new-comers started at the master's extreem left in the front row, working gradually along and back on the second and third. A regular feature of the morning's work would be the examination of homework.

The actual character of the education might be summarised as a good grounding in English, History, and elementary Mathematics with French and Latin, but in those days there was no Science.

I must refer to the valuable education (in its broader sense) derived from one's schoolfellows who were able to enlarge one's knowledge of life in general. There were sons of farmers, sons of members of the legal and medical professions and of people engaged in trade and business, a microcosm of the great world. It is in this respect that the country Grammar Schools have the advantage over the large City Schools. There seems to me a great advantage to a boy in the fact of part at least of his education being gained in the Grammar Schools. May Prescot Grammar School long continue to fill such a niche in the Country's educa-tional system as it has filled for 400 years !

2 - **F.P. Best,** M.Sc. (1908-17)

Looking back over ten years of life at school I realise that it was one long period of interest, amusement and relative lack of responsibility, and it always seems a pity that there are so few boys who can realise what a grand time they are having at school. My brother and I went to the old School just after Easter, 1908, and it was touch and go whether we went to Prescot Grammar School or Cowley School in St Helens. However the reputation of Prescot Grammar School andparticularly the hopes raised by Mr C.W.H. Richardson as Headmaster, appear to have been the things that decided our parents.

In those days there were only two masters, the Headmaster and a very pleasant young man named Proud and we were of course in the old building in High Street. Soon after our arrival the old part of the Schoolroom was divided into two sections and Mt Targett joined us as the History and Geography Master.

I remember telling my parents with some glee that I had been spanked not less than thirty-seven times in the first term, which remarkable statement was met with fowns on their part. I often feel that the religious way in which we turned out between 11 and 11-15 to get in a quarter of an hour's football practice with a tennis ball was one of the reasons why we were enabled to turn out one of the best school football teams in the area. The chief schools we played were Upholland Grammar School, the Widnes Secondary School and the St Helens Catholic Grammar School. Going to Upholland was rather a day's trip. We had an early lunch, climbed on to a brake drawn by two stout horses and were driven the 10 or 12 miles over the toip of Billinge Hill, arriving about 2-30 or 3 in the afternoon. After a good game we were always given a very good tea at Upholland School and drove back again late in the afternoon. At Prescot Cricket Club we were given the full facilities o the pavilion and I especially enjoyed those occasions when, playing the old boys, the "Old Head" would take about four or five wickets and knock up 60 runs on his own.

About 1911 or 1912 we got the first indications that an agitation was on foot for the provision of a new building but, alas, few of us realised all the processes of Local Government and practically none of us realised that the first Great War was close upon us. It is difficult to write about those four years of the war period without thinking of the large number of friends whose names are inscribed on the roll of honour. The whole of Knowsley Park seemed to be one enormous camp and a day rarely passed without some draft leaving Prescot for the front. I remember very well seeing my first military funeral and was tremendously impressed with the solemnity of the slow march to Handel's 'Dead March' in Saul

On one occasion during the chestnut season, four of us were carrying out an experiment on 'the latent heat of steam.' The Headmaster came in to check up on how we were getting on. Suddenly a terrific explosion rent the air and a chestnut blew itself to pieces on the nearby stove; but although the Headmaster was almost smothered in tiny bits of chestnut, with commendable presence of mind he continued merely to carry on the inspection of the experiment and as he left he suggested that it might be wiser to pierce a chestnut before trying to bake it----"a mere matter of allowing the gases to escape and avoiding increased pressure with temperature. Remember Charles' Law."

3 - **John Lyon,** (1917 - 1925)

Prior to my reaching the age of eight, I had been entered for the Prescot Grammar School. My father had been a pupil there in 1883 and Uncle Austin in '89 so it was not surprising that I was so registered. A vacancy having occurred, and I having reached the age of eight, I started on 2nd November, 1917. Elias, my brother, was already there and took me on that day into what was a new world.

In 1908. Charles W.H. Richardson had been appointed headmaster and the school flourished under his leadership. He was the head during the whole of my life at the school and I can assuredly say it was from him that I received, not necessarily any learning , but my true education. He was the most respected man both in and out of school. He had gathered a staff whom he moulded in his pattern, both female during the war years and subsequent thereto the male staff. One of the staff, Miss Milburn who married Mr Bailey a history master at the school, later set up a much sought-after private school in Prescot.

Prescot Grammar School in High Street consisted basically of three rooms; the first housed forms I, II and III with, adjacent, a slightly larger room occupied by forms IVb and IVa. The third room was in fact the hall divided by a curtain with Vb on one side and Va on the other. There was no staff room or headmaster's study; the head merely had a two-foot square desk about three feet six inches high at which he sat on a backless stool in the sixth-form area. In 1917 many of the staff were female and received the respect for their sex which was innate in well brought-up boys such as we were.

I sat on the front row in the 'first form', the newest of new boys. Each desk seating four had a sloping top and a shelf underneath for books and school bag. The fixed seat was joined to the desk by a cast-iron frame at either end. As I have already mentioned, the room contained the first three forms; mixed ability teaching, so often derided today, is by no means new. At that time, discipline was strict and equally exercised to all three forms regardless of the fact that they covered an age-range from eight to eleven. After Christmas, at the beginning of the spring term I moved up into the second form in which I began Latin, French and elementary algebra. At the end of the summer term each exam result was posted on the form notice board by the mistress or master responsible for each subject. Pass or fail? Great excitement; to good, exultant, rushing home to pass the news to parents and perhaps the less good being more discrete. I came top of the form and was therefore due to receive a prize. I was still then only eight years old.

The day before the prize-giving ceremony, the Hall had to be made suitable for the boys, of which there were about one hundred and fifty, and the visitors, fathers, mothers and relatives and, of course, local dignitaries All the desks were moved to the end of the room and suitably stacked in tiers to form a sort of gallery on which the boys were to sit. The big boys of the Vth and VIth forms constituted the majority of the work-force and a small boy of eight was required only to keep out of the way. I gazed speechless at the feverish activity and the skill with which these huge fellows of sixteen to eighteen handled those desks to construct a stable auditorium. I recall that I suffered one disillusion.

The gallery had been built and there was a lull in the activity so I was flattered when one of the big boys invited me to try the seating on the top tier with him. Off he went and I gladly followed, his longer legs getting him to the top when I was only half-way up. However, I persevered and finally reached my goal. He patted the seat beside him and down I sat. To my dismay he had placed an upturned drawing pin in a strategic place. It was, I think, my first experience of the duplicity of one's fellow men. I have never forgotten the headmaster, later in my school life, quoting, "..........beware of Greeks bearing gifts".

I remember little of the prize-giving except the moment in due course when I proceeded to the front to receive my prize, *Bonnie Prince Charlie* by GA Henty which I have beside me as I write, its book-plate with the Prescot coat of arms, *FLOREAT PRESCOTIA* , and the words printed in Gothic "Prescot Grammar School - Prize awarded to J. Lyon, Form II, 1st Prize Midsummer 1918, C.W.H. Richardson, Headmaster". Is it unseemly of me to look back and feel proud of that eight-year-old me? I would wish, with Wordsworth, that "the child is father of the man".

4 - C.P. Maynard, (1921 - 28)

Being a pupil during the last days of the School at the old building in High Street and, for some time afterwards, at the new in St Helens Road, it may be of interest to recall some of the people and events at this interesting period in the long history of the school. To overcome the difficulty of accommodation in the High

Street premises, classes were held also in the Assembly Rooms near Mr W.A. Cross's office, the Parish Rooms and in the Sunday School in the street across from the Kings Arms. With each of these 'scattered' schools I associate certain masters or mistresses. At the Parish Rooms we had Miss Huckle, Miss Bufton and, I think, Miss Milburn. Messrs Robinson and Hammond I remember at the Assembly Rooms and Mr Stevenson at the Sunday School. "Richy," or "Dick," as Mr C.W.H.Richardson was so disrespectfully known from Sixth Former to junior boy, reigned supremely over all with Mr Whitworth as second-in-command. Mr Richardson was a most forceful character who awed me from the first day until the last. That high, clerical Cambridge collar fascinated me. Later in the new school, to hear that heavy tread in the distance or the loud voice booming round the corridors was lways a signal for complete rectitude and silence throughout the whole edifice. To sit on the front row of a class during the Headmaster's Latin or Mathematics lessons was an ordeal from which I thought I would never recover. There were few, too, who did the "Bend Over" exercise in his study without realising that the Head had an excellent understanding of juvenile psychology.

The boys of my time are scattered far and wide now. Maybe some will read these lines and, like me, recall with pleasure the days and faces of those bygone times. To the School today, on behalf of all those who were once there, may I say, "Good Luck and Success to you all and long may the old School flourish."

5 - F.T.Wainwright, B.A.,Ph.D., F.S.A. (1930-35)

One may recall the morning groups for prayers, in 1930 in the corridor and in 1935 around the new Hall; the daily ordeal of the Latin lesson in the Third and Fourth Forms; sandwich lunches in an empty classroom and, later, meals in the new dining hall with determined manoeuverings for second helpings. There was the deathly silence during examinations; the crazy football of Founder's Day with the two halves of the school locked in mortal combat; the rivalry of House matches and the inevitable athletic supremacy of the Omegas.

We spent many hours lifting and balancing with one hand a chair weighted with an increasing number of dictionaries; Logan Armour, huge but very gentle, set a very high standard. Hand over fist we worked a perilous way along the iron bar which spanned the Sixth Form Room. At least a dozen minds will always hold the memory of C.G. Forster (later Principal of Wigan Technical College) swinging wildly with one hand flailing and crying loudly for help while heavy footsteps approached along the corridor.

One should not forget "Timmie" the boisterous and friendly dog, now gone to his long rest and it is difficult to remember the school without the heavy footsteps, the booming greeting and the buttonhole flower of "Timmie's" master, the great "Richy," who figures in so many memories.

6 - **W.E.W. Smith.** (1934-44)

The one really big change in the staff took place in 1937 when the Headmaster, Mr C.W.H. Richardson, retired and Mr R. Spencer Briggs was appointed. A change in our leadership had been half expected for a short time before but the boys had not given much thought to the matter, probably because of the Coronation celebrations which, like the Silver Jubilee celebrations of King George V in 1935, took up everyone's attention.

The last six years have been very trying times for everybody owing to the war, but even before 1939 the school was set a very difficult problem as people were beginning to think more about secondary education.as a result our school, like so many others, was faced with a problem which was by no means easy to solve. More boys wanted to come to the school, mainly from the growing Huyton area, whilst accommodation was very strictly limited. Consequently the school lost its truly local atmosphere. The situation became worse when members of the staff were called to the colours at the outbreak of the present conflict. (World War II)

The school grounds have been radically altered in these ten years. In my early days I remember the groundsman and his assistants using small four-wheeled trucks to carry earth along a light railway to level the sports field. More changes took place at the outbreak of war when air-raid shelters were constructed. The senior boys helped to prepare for the foundations. A large area of ground was put under cultivation and on it boys now have their own allotments where some fine produce is grown. The two farm camps, two prefects' dances and the winning of the Liverpool Schools' Shield have all lent an atmosphere of pleasure to recent school life.

The fact that the school has survived for four hundred years and grown in strength from year to year is evidence of its usefulness and purpose and it has every appearance of still further progress in the years to come.

7 - Professor **David Wilcock,** (1952-1959)

Recollections of my days at Prescot fuse into a blur and I do not know that I can get the chronology right. I recall playing chaotic games of football in the playground with a tennis ball (at all ages between 11 and 16) the game I was involved in being just one of many going on at the same time. I can't recall playing in the playground as a sixth-former. Perhaps adolescent dignity got the better of natural inclination! Dinner-time figures prominently in my recollections for some reason. Lunchtime meals were taken at 12.30 or 1.00 pm in a white-walled one-storey building approached by a narrow passage between the woodwork room and the main building. Hurricanes blowing through this narrow passage could stop you in your tracks and rain "coming down in stair-rods" could drench you before you were able to enter the refectory. Mr Hawthorne presided over the lunchtime cacophony during my days at school, always with an affable authority which was seldom challenged.

A room overlooking the school cricket pitch at the rear of the school was my first form room, 3B1 my first form and Mr Dixon my first form master. The only 'dedicated' rooms in those days were those for chemistry (Mr Bramall contrived some wonderful experiments with what I now realize were very inadequate resources), physics, geography and woodwork. I recall proudly making a stool under the watchful eye of Mr Davis and taking it home for my mother. Held together by faith and vast quantities of resinous, heavily aromatic glue, it graced our house for several years. Miss Berisford was my first geography teacher but I also have very clear memories of Mr Stevenson's freehand maps drawn on the blackboard with effortless accuracy. Peter Harvey, one of the younger, more informal teachers in the 1950's was my last geography master and I recall with affection and appreciation the long discussions we had with him during sixth-form classes in the Library.

My elder brother passed through the school four years earlier than I and prepared me fot eh distinctive teahing methods eployed by some of the teachers. Mr Charles Middlehurst was renowned for his acerbic wit.

"This boy does well to remain anonymous", he would say of an essay handed in without a name. "I want this essay handed in next Tuesday, which I see from my diary is the date of the new moon. I shall therefore expect more than the usual crop of lunacy."

Some of these witticisms, I suspect, have by now been recycled several times the length and breadth of the United Kingdom. I also remember Charles because for two or three years on Saturday mornings he gave me a lift in his car to all the 'away' fixtures of the senior football team of which I was a member. The 1952 and 1953 enrolments proved to contain many fine footballers and I would love to know where some of them are now. Under the captaincy of Phil Morgan we won the junior and senior school shields, I think, the finals of which were played at Anfield before the 'glory days' of Liverpool F.C. During many televised programmes from Anfield in later years I have tortured my sons with exaggerated stories of how I played on that hallowed turf.

Other recollections include those of assemblies in the open-air quadrangle on fine summer mornings; walking through Prescot to church on Founder's Day; the anarchic ritual of Founder's Day football; going home to Eccleston on the No 93 bus from Hope Street. In middle life I often think of my generation as perhaps the luckiest of all in terms of the opportunities we have had. We missed war and conscription - just. We enjoyed the early and maturing benefits of the 1944 Education Act. Unemployment was not three million when we looked for jobs. I count as one of my specific pieces of good fortune that I attended Prescot Grammar School when I did.

8 - Douglas J. Bridson, M.B.A., M.C.I.P.S. (1961 - 1968)

Reflecting on life at Prescot Grammar School during what came to be known as the *swinging sixties*, I am struck by the contrast between the traditions and heritage of a four-hundred-year-old grammar school and the pace of change in all aspects of life which that decade witnessed.

My first trip abroad was in 1963 when the school arranged a student exchange to Amsterdam and we travelled in a DC3 Dakota - a relic of the war, no doubt. By the end of the decade, Concorde had made its maiden flight and man had landed on the moon !

The School, and certain members of staff in particular, struggled to maintain the uniform and dress code: Beatle-style hair-cuts and cuban-soled shoes were definitely not appreciated and pupils 'stretched staff tolerance' to the limit. Messrs Middlehurst and Burrows were especially unappreciative of the modern style.

The sixties was the period during which the cities of Liverpool and Manchester, with Prescot tucked neatly in between, dominated both the 'pop' music scene and the national sport - soccer. I recall on many occasions leaving school at the end of the day to go straight to queue for tickets or to attend a Wednesday evening game. Prescot Grammar School played its part by regularly winning the Inter-Schools Cup.

Former pupils of the period may well recall the Prefects' Dance of 1966 which was almost a disaster because it co-incided with one of England's World Cup matches. Several 'runners' from the upper sixth were compelled to visit the local 'pub', The Soldier, to keep check on the score.

The new Hall was opened during this period and the school put it to good use with regular cinema evenings to compliment the more traditional P.G.S. entertainments of Joe Kirk's musical evenings or the school plays.

Like many others, one did one's bit by singing in the school choir but I have particularly fond memories of Mr Roberts' 'spectacular' production of *A Man for All Seasons* in 1967. The Prescot Reporter commented, "P.G.S. productions have always been noted for their striking sets and stage effects" and commended the school for its courage in producing a play which was currently enjoying both West-end stage and film success. This was all the more memorable when one considers that the female characters were portrayed by 2nd and 3rd formers - fraternisation with the girl's school being still somewhat distant.

Other memories of the period range from playground years during the Cuban missile crisis and the Kennedy assassination to heated debate in the sixth-form Economics class at the time of Harold Wilson's famous Sterling devaluation.

Throughout this turbulent decade, P.G.S. provided a sense of stability and continuity which I feel was most manifestly demonstrated each year at the traditional Founder's Day service at Prescot Parish Church.

Like many of my contemporaries, I recognise that the teaching staff and the P.G.S. culture established the foundation for subsequent academic and career achievement.

9 - **Malcolm Tyrer,** M.B.,Ch.B., M.R.C.G.P. (1973 - 1980)

My primary school headmaster had given wise counsel concerning the transition to grammar school life "..........no longer a big fish in a little pond........." On a cold grey September morning, chaperoned by my cousin about to start his second year, I entered the school and joined the other minnows of One Omega to meet our new form master. Mr Tarbuck was as fresh to the staff-room as we were to the playground and was far less formal than we had all feared. In time a foundation was laid that would stand the turmoil of maturing years, rocked by the upheaval of some of the greatest changes our school would see in its 400 year history.

I recall Mr Kirby's prodigious memory for names in music classes; the charming didactism of Mr 'Sparky' Watts; the accurate aim of Mr Thomas with marked English essays and that of Mr Roberts with a piece of chalk propelled at French lesson provocateurs.

By 1975, the boys' and girls' grammar schools amalgamated, little seemed to have changed at first. Somehow, the girls existed 'over there' (amongst them my future wife) and we were 'over here'. Yet we soon learned to tread the path between Lathum and Park Wings. The girls did not like us at first. They were prim, proper, mature and disciplined. We were risky, less certain and with an occasionally scruffy, embryonic idea of masculinity. This was never better demonstrated than by the sight of the sexes divided, as if by an iron curtain as real as the Berlin Wall, at the end-of-year disco in 1976. Similar events in subsequent years proved a good deal more successful and perhaps charted a positive shift in the self identity of the new co-educational school.

The professionalism of the head and staff were soon to be tested when, in the months of February and June 1978, two fires caused major damage at Lathum Wing. Many valuable artifacts were lost including the rolls of honour commemorating the Old Boys of the School who had fallen in two world wars.The same year saw the opening of a new sixth-form centre at Park Wing where the pleasant surroundings and excellent facilities allowed A-level pupils to forge a very real sense of communal purpose. I recall many lively debates, formal and informal, in an atmosphere of growing confidence and awareness. Many of the teaching staff supported a scheme in which sixth-formers assisted with first and second year classes. This helped to develop communication, understanding and respect between pupils from the two sites.

All too soon, my time at Prescot Grammar School came to an end: perhaps the best years of my life ? Certainly they had been happy ones during which I had developed in knowledge and character. The School itself had stood the test of change and it continued to achieve at the highest levels in all respects.

10 - **Patricia McAuley** - 2nd year Medical Student. (1984 - 89)

The youngest of four, all of whom went to Prescot School, gave me many preconceptions about this long-standing establishment. There still remained teachers who had taught my brother 14 years previously.

The First and Second Years were based at Lathum Wing, a less foreboding site in the eyes of a first-year than the larger Park Wing. Its strange array of buildings gave to certain areas of the site characters of their own. The Spencer Briggs building stood proud above the rest and contained the science laboratories where many an experiment had gone wrong as one listened to the sounds of games from the sports fields below.

In the woodwork building, a tall quiet Mr Davis could, with a puff of his dignifying pipe, transform your split piece of wood into an object of some usefulness which was worth taking home. The English departments were always more peaceful and relaxed. The additonal pleasures of drama and library time made the subject appear rather like a break than a difficult academic subject. Tucked away at the side of Lathum Wing was the art building. Here Mr Hudson would relate the most interesting stories which inevitably incurred the jealousy of fellow pupils.

During the first year, along with several other girls in the form and accompanied by two members of staff, I went to the outdoor pursuits base at Dent in the Yorkshire dales. Crowded into a mini-bus we formed such a heavy load that the vehicle was prevented from climbing some of the hills and we were forced to walk behind. Dent was an erie place and having a grave-yard as a back-garden caused our imaginations to run wild particularly when, in the intense darkness, a floor-board creaked spontaneously. Three days of exercise, rain and burnt dinners left one tired out but with many a tale to tell.

Formal occasions in the second year were something of an experience. The annual Founder's Day service in Prescot Parish Church caused one to feel part of the past and a member of a historic institution with the opportunity to tread in the footsteps of generations of former scholars. The annual Carol Service in the Methodist Church was a joyous occasion which marked not only the birth of Christ but also the end of term and commencement of school holidays.

Examination time was unforgettable; one remembers revision lessons when the realisation dawned that a tremendous amount of work was still to be covered. The rows of desks filling the hall at Park Wing echoed to the nervous chatter of friends reeling off trigonometry formulae and French verbs.

Eventually the great day came when, with relief and yet a new expectancy of university life, we put down our pens for the last time at Prescot School.

EVENTS IN THE HISTORY OF
PRESCOT GRAMMAR SCHOOL & PRESCOT SCHOOL
1544 - 1994

1509	Preference given to boys from the parish of Prescot by the founders of Brasenose College, Oxford.
1544	10th October. School 'foundyt' in the will of Gilbert Lathum, Archdeacon of Man.
1547	Reference to the 'scholehowse' in the records of Prescot court leet.
1592	Survey of the manor states that the School was on the site of the present Post Office in Church Street.
1684	Eccleston School (Seddon's Cottage) erected on Eccleston Hill.
1759	The School was moved from the 'Post Office site'
1760	into a new building in High Street near its junction with St Helens Road. This building remained in use until 1924 and then was used as a school clinic for many years. Demolished c. 1990.
1809	Boarders were being taken.
1924	New wooden building opened on St Helens Road site.
1930	New hall / gymnasium opened.
1933	Grant of Arms
1938	Further extensions including new laboratories.
1955	Phase 1. New buildings opened in Knowsley Park Lane for newly founded Prescot Girls' Grammar School..
1960	Phase 2 buildings opened on 'Park' Site.
1964	Spencer Briggs buildings opened on St Helens Road, 'Lathum', site.
1975	Amalgamation of Boys' and Girls' Schools.
1977	Sixth Form block and Technology extension at Park Site.
1978	Disastrous fires at Lathum Site, February & July.
1985	Extension to Craft / Technology block, Park Site.
1992	Wooden buildings demolished on Lathum site.
1993	Extension to Park Site and complete closure of Lathum Site proposed.

□□□

HEADMASTERS OF THE SCHOOL
1544 - 1994

Many of the earlier Masters are unknown and others only known from casual references. Foster's Alumni Oxonienses and Venn's Alumni Cantabrigienses afford additional information in some cases. Research pre-1944 by F.A.Bailey.

Thomas WEBSTER, c. 1587

William FLETCHER, c. 1605-8, of Hart Hall, Oxford, matric. 1602.

Devereux BEVERLEY, c. 1613, of King's, Cambridge, M.A.,1612,Vicar of Eastham,Chesh,1615

----- BOYER, c. 1614.

Richard TYRER, c. 1627, of Brasenose, Oxford, B.A., 1621. Was also Curate of Prescot.

Thomas DOMVILLE, c. 1647.

Henry SHAW, c. 1663.

John LEIGH, c. 1667.

----- BRIARLEY, 1647-9. Probably James Briarley, of Christ's, Cambridge, B.A.,1673-4, b. at Nantwich, 1648 and d. at Manchester, 1682.

John LODGE, appointed July, 1679. Probably John Lodge, of Queen's, Oxford, B.A., 1675, a native of Bolton-le-Sands, Lancashire.

Nathaniel COOPER, 1685-8, of Brasenose, Oxford, B.A., 1683, a native of Runcorn.

Henry WARING, 1688-1725. Buried at Prescot, 19th June, 1725.

Rev. Robert CHAPMAN, c. 1731-49. Perhaps the Rev. Robert Chapman, Curate of Burtonwood, 1716-57, who married Alice Leafe, of Prescot in 1729.

John ROBINSON, c. 1754. Perhaps John Robinson, of Christ's, Cambridge, B.A., 1744-5, a native of Lancashire.

Rev. Abraham ASHCROFT, c. 1759-85. Was also Curate of Prescot. Buried at Prescot, 23rd December, 1785. His son, James, matriculated at Brasenose in 1786.

----- REDHEAD, c.1786. Probably Timothy Redhead (see below)

Rev. William ELLAM, c. 1793-1808. He resigned his mastership in 1808.

Timothy REDHEAD, 1808-13.

John HAMNETT, 1813-49. buried at Prescot, 27th October, 1849, aged 74.

Rev. Haygarth Taylor BAINES, 1851-62, of Christ's, Cambridge, M.A., 1850. Born at Satterthwaite, Lancs. Chaplain of Prescot Union, 1857-62. Headmaster, Hawkshead Grammar School. 1862-81. Died at Sawrey, Lancs., 1908.

Rev. John Cooper WOOD, 1862-4, of St John's, Cambridge, M.A.

Rev. Charles J.S. WALKER, 1864-7, of St John's, Cambridge, M.A.

J. MACINTOSH, 1867-70.

Edward LAWLER, 1871-82.

John SCHOLFIELD, 1882-1907, London University.

Charles W.H. RICHARDSON, 1908-37, of Sidney Sussex, Cambridge, M.A., and London,B.Sc. Formerly senior mathematical master, Trent College, Derbyshire. b. Yorkshire. c. 1872, d. Great Driffield, Yorkshire.

R. Spencer BRIGGS, 1937-63, of St Catharine's, Cambridge, M.A. Formerly assistant master, Liverpool Collegiate, senior modern languages master, Cambridge and County High School. b. Carlisle. d. Ormskirk, May 1964. Buried at Carlisle.

Michael J.M. BROWN, 1963-67, of Emmanuel, Cambridge, M.A., of St Peter's, Oxford, M.A.Formerly taught at Wrekin College, Reading School and Wallasey Grammar School.

John C.S. WEEKS, 1968-77, of St Catharine's, Cambridge, M.A. Formerly assistant teacher, Ipswich School; Head of Geography, Royal Grammar School, HighWycombe; C.B.E., 1991.

Peter A. BARLOW, 1977--, of the University of Leeds, B.A. and B.Mus., and of the University of Cambridge, P.G.C.E. Formerly assistant master, Langley Park School, Bromley and Manchester Grammar School; Deputy Headteacher, Highfield School, Wolverhampton.

BENEFACTORS OF THE SCHOOL

The following rendered outstanding service to the School or were very substantial donors to the Endowments and Funds..

Gilbert LATHUM, M.A., B.D.,Archdeacon of Man. (Bequest for the foundation of a Free Grammar School at Prescot, 1544.)

His Majesty KING EDWARD VI. (Grant of the funds of the chantry gilds.)

The Right Hon. Henry, fourth EARL of DERBY, K.G. (He took the school under his special protection and saved it from almost certain extinction, 1587-92. As Steward of Prescot he authorised the school to receive rents of houses built on the waste land of the manor).

The PROVOST and SCHOLARS of King's College, Cambridge. (Granted 10 shillings a year for 20 years, 1592-1612, and, as lords of the manor, sanctioned the grant of rents of houses built on the waste.)

Thomas MEAD, M.A., Vicar of Prescot. (He was instrumental in securing the support of the Provost of King's College and of the Earl of Derby, 1587-92, thus saving the school. He acted as overseer of the school for many years and restored its finances,)

Robert PLUMPTON. (Granted the site of the original school-house in Church Street.

Robert CONNEY. (Granted rent charges in Prescot and Rainhill, c. 1600).

Richard HAWARDEN. (Bequest of land in Cumber Lane, Whiston, 1600).

Elizabeth GLOVER. (Granted rents of houses in Prescot, c. 1610).

John ALCOCK. (Bequest of £48, 1653).

Abraham BALL, M.A., Vicar of Prescot. (Residuary bequest, 1677).

Thomas GLOVER. (Granted a yearly rent of £2 on the Mill Hill House in Prescot, 1690).

Ellen SIDDALL. (Bequest of £48, 1729).

Basil Thomas ECCLESTON. (Granted the site on Hackley Moss for the rebuilding of the school, 1729).

William LAWTON. (Granted the residue of Lyon's charity in Upton-in-Widnes, 1762).

John WYKE. (Bequest of £100, 1787).

Samuel SEWELL, M.A., Vicar of Prescot. (Bequest of £200, 1815).

Elizabeth ATHERTON. (Bequest of £300. 1828).

Canon Harry MITCHELL, M.A., Vicar of Prescot. (Chairman of the Governors for 32 years, 1887-1919 Largely through his efforts the closing of the school was prevented in 1904-6).

G. Hinde NISBETT, J.P. (Bequest of £100 to the Prize Fund, 1921.)

Anne DRIFFIELD. (Bequest of £150 to the Prize Fund, 1924.)

George QUICK. (Contingent legacy to the Prize Fund, 1929.)

The PROVOST and FELLOWS of King's College, Cambridge.

The PRINCIPAL and FELLOWS of Brazenose College, Oxford.

The DIRECTORS of BRITISH INSULATED CALLENDER'S CABLES Limited.

Frederick HALSALL. (Bequest to the Prize Fund)

John E HAWTHORNE

Annie CHANT. (Bequest to the Prize Fund - the Herbert Chant History Prize.)

Robert Spencer BRIGGS.

Rose Mary EVANS.

Sarah Elizabeth ROBINSON.

Canon O L MARTIN, M.A., Vicar of Prescot. (Chairman of Governors)

Research to 1929 by F.A. Bailey.

Records of further gifts and bequests cannot be traced and may have been destroyed in the fires of 1978.

J.S.B.

THE ARMS

LETTERS PATENT for Armorial Bearings for Prescot Grammar School, Lancashire, granted by Garter, Clarenceux and Norroy of the College of Arms, London, to the Governing Body on the twenty-fourth day of April, A.D. 1933.

TO ALL and singular to whom these Presents shall come, Sir Gerald Woods Wollaston, Knight Member of the Royal Victorian Order, Garter Principal King of Arms, Arthur William Steuart Cochrane, Esquire, Commander of the Royal Victorian Order, Clarenceux, King of Arms and Algar Henry Stafford, Esquire, upon whom has been conferred the Decoration of the Military Cross, Norroy, King of Arms, send Greeting.

WHEREAS William Arthur Cross, Solicitor of the Supreme Court of Judicature in England and Secretary to the *Prescot Grammar School* in the County Palatine of Lancaster, represented to the Most Noble Bernard Marmaduke, Duke of Norfolk, Earl Marshal and Hereditary Marshal of England, that a Grammar School at Prescot in the County Palatine of Lancaster was founded under a bequest contained in the will of Gilbert Lathum, Archdeacon of Man, dated the tenth day of October, one thousand five hundred and forty-four and proved on the first day of June, one thousand five hundred and fifty-two. That the said School now known as Prescot Grammar School is managed by a Governing Body appointed in accordance with a scheme framed by the Board of Education under the Endowed Schools Acts, 1869, 1873 and 1874, for the amendment of the Scheme regulating the Prescot Grammar School, and approved by His Majesty in Council on the twenty-eighth day of November, One thousand nine hundred and fourteen.

THAT the said Governing Body is desirous that the fit and proper Armorial Bearings should be granted and assigned for the use of the said School and he therefore on behalf of the said Governing Body of the Prescot Grammar School requested the favour of His Grace's Warrant for our granting and assigning such Armorial Bearings as might be proper to be borne and used by the said Governong Body for its use and of the said School on Seals, Shields or otherwise according to the Laws of Arms.

AND FORASMUCH as the said Earl Marshal did by Warrant under his hand and seal bearing the date the twenty-seventh day of February last authorize and direct Us to grant and assign such Armorial Ensigns accordingly : know ye therefore We the said Garter, Clarenceux and Norroy in pursuance of His Grace's Warrant and by virtue of the Letters Patent of Our Several Offices to each of us respectively granted do by these Presents grant and assign unto the Governing Body of Prescot Grammar School the Arms following, that is to say : *Or an open book proper edged gules on a chief indented azure three plates* and for the Crest *on a wreath of the colours an eagle wings elevated and addorsed or supporting with the dexter claw a torch erect gules fired proper* as the same are in the margin hereof more plainly depicted to be borne and used for ever hereafter by the said School on Seals, Shields or otherwise according to the Laws of Arms : *In witness* whereof We the said Garter, Clarenceux and Norroy, Kings of Arms have to these Presents subscribed our names and affixed the seals of our several Offices this twenty-fourth day of April in the twenty-third year of the Reign of our Sovereign Lord George the Fifth by the Grace of God of Great Britain, Ireland and the British Dominions beyond the Seas, King, Defender of the Faith, etc., and in the year of Our Lord One thousand nine hundred and thirty-three.

Gerald W. Wollaston	Arthur Cochrane	Algar Howard
Garter	*Clarenceux*	*Norroy*

ROLL OF HONOUR

Futuram Civitatem Inquirimus

Past Pupils of the School who gave their lives in two World Wars

1914 - 1918

N Beardmore	A W Johnson	J Stead
G E Broad	W J Lowe	J Tyrer
J M Clements	T P Prescott	H R Vercoe
J Copple	T S Preston	A Watkinson
R A France	W A Range	A Wensby
T R Gleave	D F Roberts	H G Whitaker
B C Green		H E Wood

1939 - 1945

Eric R Atherton	Harry Burrows	Louis B Murray
John Barker	J Godfrey Case	Thomas R Prescott
Stanley Barnes	Ernest A Collis MC	Rodney Russell
William R Barton	Thomas W Corns	Eric J Smith
Edward Bayley	Ian K Crawford	J Alfred Smith
Thomas W Beard	George A Crompton	James Shutes
John S Birch	William A T Day	Ronald Taylor
Edward Blackburn	Bernard A Finney	Ivor H Thomas
Tom Bone	Harry Gore	Thomas H Topping
James Booth	Charles G Griffiths	Alan A Turtill
William J H Boots	Wilbert D Heap	James L Whittaker
Harold St J Brodrick-Pittard MC	Robert Hughes	Sam J Whittingham DFM
Robert A Brodrick-Pittard	John Kerr	W Edward Williams
John Burns	James F Lea	William Woods
	Hector N McNeil	

We will remember them.

□□□

The names of the fallen were inscribed on two panels affixed to the corridor wall immediately inside the entrance of the 1924 building in St Helens Road. They were both lost at the time of the fire. Certainly one was burned; it was said that the other was salvaged but later stolen. Former pupils, many of them school-fellows of those who fell, contributed to a replacement memorial to be placed in the foyer of the Knowsley Lane building during the 450th Anniversary year, 1994.

□□□

Some published works of
F. A. BAILEY

Books

A History of Southport.   (Downie, 1955)   (reprinted, Sefton Libraries, 1992)
Prescot Parish Church : Historical Notes, revised edition.   (Brit. Publ. 1960)

Articles

The Court Leet of Prescot		(H.S., Vol. 84, 1932)
Coroner's inquests held in the Manor of Prescot, 1746-89		(H.S., Vol. 86, 1934)
Prescot Grammar School in Elizabethan times.		(H.I.., Vol. 86, 1934)
The minutes of the trustees of the turnpike roads		
from Liverpool to Prescot, 1726-89.	Part 1	(H.S., Vol. 88, 1936)
ditto	Part 2	(H.S., Vol. 89, 1937)
An ancient Prescot font.		(H.S., Vol. 89, 1937)
"Bergerode".		(H.S., Vol. 89, 1937)
A certificate of burial in woollen, 1682.		(H.S., Vol. 89, 1937)
A fragment of the original parish register of Prescot, 1538-41.		(H.S., Vol. 90, 1938)
A Norris deed relating to Prescot, 1286.		(H.S., Vol. 91, 1939)
An indenture of apprenticeship, 1535.		
The churchwardens' accounts of Prescot, 1523-1607.	Part 1	(H.S., Vol. 92, 1940)
A Neolithic axe found at Whiston, 1941.		(H.S., Vol. 93, 1941)
The churchwardens' accounts of Prescot, 1523-1607.	Part 2	(H.S., Vol. 95, 1943)
Early coalmining in Prescot, Lancashire.		(H.S., Vol. 99, 1947)
Some memoranda by William Moore, Esq.,		
concerning Liverpool and Walton.		(H.S., Vol. 100, 1948)
Notes on the history of Southport.		
IN N.A.H.T. Jubilee Conference Souvenir, 1947.		
The Elizabethan playhouse in Prescot, Lancashire.		(H.S., Vol. 103, 1951)
The origin and growth of Southport.		
IN Town Planning Review.		Vol. 21, No.4, 1951)
An old watchmaker's workshop.		
IN Trans. of the Ancient Monuments Soc., 1953.		

Works edited by F.A. Bailey.

CHURCHWARDENS' accounts of Prescot, Lancashire, 1523-1697	(R.S., Vol. 104)
FARNWORTH, St Luke's Church.	
The register of Farnworth Chapel, 1538-1612	(L.R.P.S., 1941)
HUYTON, St Michael's and All Angels' Church.	
The parish register of Huyton, 1578-1727.	(L.R.P.S., 1946)
SELECTION from the Prescot Court Leet	
and other records, 1447-1600.	(R.S., 1937)

*This list compiled and published by permission
of the County Librarian of Lancashire, Preston.*

Index

Although not exhaustive, the index contains all leading and many secondary references.

Names in heavy type refer to recorded **Benefactors** of the School.

Italicised entries direct the reader to the *Appendix.*